Find What You Want on the Internet

Mark Neely

NET.WORKS

Net.Works, PO Box 200
Harrogate, N.Yorks
HG1 2YR   England

http://www.net-works.co.uk
Email: sales@net-works.co.uk
UK Fax: 01423-526035

Net.Works is an imprint of Take That Ltd.

Published in association with Maximedia Pty Ltd
PO Box 529 Kiama, NSW 2533, Australia.

ISBN: 1 873668 48 1

© 1998 Take That Ltd. & Maximedia Pty Ltd

All rights reserved around the world. This publication is copyright and may not be reproduced, in whole or in part, in any manner (except for excerpts thereof for bona fide purposes in accordance with the Copyright Act) without the prior consent in writing from the Publisher.

10 9 8 7 6 5 4 3 2 1

Trademarks:
Trademarked names are used throughout this book. Rather than place a trademark symbol in every occurance of a trademark name, the names are being used only in an editorial fashion for the benefit of the trademark owner, with no intention to infringe the trademark.

Printed and bound in The United Kingdom

Disclaimer:
The information in this book is distributed on an "as is" basis, without warranty. While very effort has been made to ensure that this book is free from errors or omissions, neither the author, the publisher, or their respective employees and agents, shall have any liability to any person or entity with respect to any liability, loss or damage caused or alleged to have been caused directly or indirectly by advice or instructions contained in this book or by the computer hardware or software products described herein. **Readers are urged to seek prior expert advice before making decisions, or refraining from making decisions, based on information or advice contained in this book.**

Throughout this book you will find web addresses on various subjects. These will start you off on your journey around the WWW. However, just like 'real life' addresses, some may have changed since going to press. We hope this does not spoil your enjoyment.

Contents

Introduction - Searching the Net 4
1. What is the Web? 8
2. The Virtual Library 14
3. The Information Chase 18
4. The Anatomy of a Search Engine 25
5. Information Retrieval Concepts 30
6. Yahoo! 34
7. AltaVista 38
8. Excite 42
9. HotBot 46
10. WebCrawler 50
11. Lycos 53
12. InfoSeek 58
13. Meta-Search Engines 62
14. Intelligent Search Agents 71
15. Finding Someone Online 80
16. Other Research Options 86
Appendix - Search Engines and Software 103

Introduction

Searching the Net

Even without the benefit of hindsight, it's easy to see why the World Wide Web has attracted so much attention in recent years.

Not since the advent of the printing press has humankind wielded such a powerful communications tool. Almost overnight, it seems, we were given unlimited access to a global, electronic publishing medium that - unlike earlier forms of mass communication - contains few formal barriers to entry. Individuals and corporations alike can now make information available to the masses.

The World Wide Web has been heralded as a boon for education and research communities, as it provides efficient and cost-effective access to a variety of information sources around the globe.

The changing face of information dissemination

Students, researchers and individuals now have access to up-to-the-minute news, weather information, sports results, editorial and opinion columns, articles and research papers - even entire books are available online. Library catalogues, index systems, government databases and public records are rapidly making the transition from paper to electronic storage.

Access to any public information or news service is now as close as your PC. It's all there - and most of it is available free or at minimal cost.

Yet, paradoxically, it is the staggering volume of information available online and the unprecedented growth rate of the Internet's information resources that have the potential to *cripple* this embryonic medium before its full power can be realised.

The information challenge

The scope of information available online is mind-boggling. Yet, because it has been collected and distributed in such a non-structured manner, attempts to locate information can be frustratingly fruitless - unless you are adept at finding your way around cyberspace.

Beating the information blues

This book is designed primarily to teach readers how to use the World Wide Web and its many search tools **efficiently**.

It will introduce readers to principles that guide information gathering on the Web, as well as focus on search tools that enhance productivity and efficiency. The vast amount of information generated each day via Usenet (Internet news) and email mailing lists will also be examined, including how you can tap into these to find what you want.

This book in a nutshell

→ Chapter 1 contains a **brief overview** of the World Wide Web, and introduces you to some basic concepts used throughout this book. Readers who are familiar with the Web can skip this chapter.

→ Chapter 2 discusses the **evolution** of the Internet (in particular the Web) as a virtual online reference source for research.

→ Chapter 3 examines the **Internet as an information resource**, and highlights skills Web users can learn to harness its power.

→ Chapter 4 introduces **Search Engines**, including their origin and how they operate.

→ Judging the **"authoritative" value of Internet resources** is discussed in Chapter 5, an especially important concern for young readers developing information analysis skills.

→ Chapters 6 to 12 contain **in-depth reviews** of the most popular and powerful Search Engines, namely Yahoo!, AltaVista, Excite, HotBot, ANZWERS, WebCrawler, Lycos and InfoSeek.

→ **Meta-Search Engines**, and the advantages they offer, are discussed in Chapter 13.

→ Chapter 14 looks to the future, when smart software tools known as **Intelligent Search Agents** will tailor searches to your needs.

→ Chapter 15 contains useful hints and tips on the vexing issue of how to **find someone's email address**.

→ Finally, in Chapter 16 we review often **overlooked Internet resources**, including Usenet newsgroups and email discussion groups.

→ The Appendix contains a **list of Web sites and search tools** that readers can use to further explore the online world.

How to use this book

This book aims to introduce the reader to using the Internet as a research tool, with particular emphasis on World Wide Web Search Engines. It is not designed as a thorough introduction to the principles of networking, specific Internet resources or the Internet in general. Instead, it is aimed at those who already have some experience using the Internet and the World Wide Web, and wish to hone their Internet research skills.

In writing this book and preparing the examples and screen shots, I have focused mainly on Windows-based software. However, the general principles outlined are applicable to all Internet users, whether accessing via Macintosh or Windows-based PCs - or any other flavours in-between.

In short, this book aims to help you use your Internet time more effectively by introducing you to the world of Internet search tools.

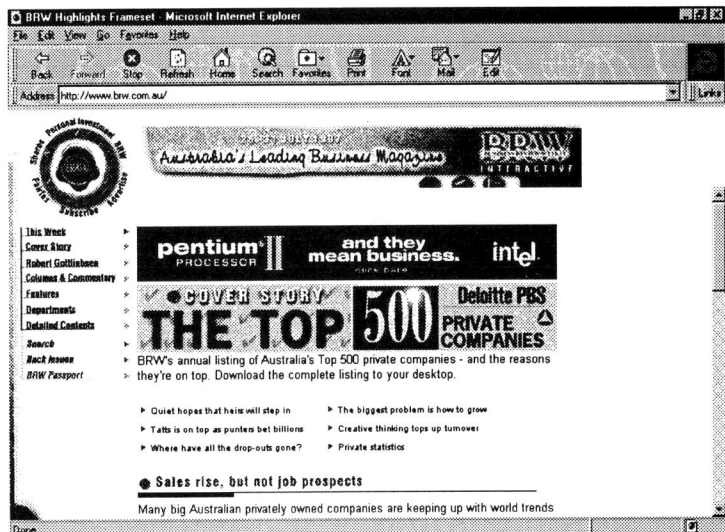

Contacting me

Please feel free to contact me via my publisher with comments:

sales@net-works.co.uk

Alternatively, you can email me direct at:

accessnt@ozemail.com.au

To learn more about specific aspects of the Internet and the World Wide Web, please look out for other books from Net.Works.

The Complete Beginner's Guide to the Internet and *Complete Beginner's Guide to the World Wide Web* will help you learn more about the basics of the Internet.

The Internet Guide for Teachers, Students & Parents shows you how to get the most from the Internet as an educational resource, and is especially useful for parents and teachers who want their charges to become "Internet-aware".

Entrepreneurs will find *The Complete Beginner's Guide to Making Money on the Internet* and *The Experts Business Guide to the Internet* useful, as they explain how to use the Internet to your advantage in business - saving time and increasing profits.

(For more information and an order form see pages 109-112.)

Chapter 1

What is the Web?

The World Wide Web (WWW or Web for short) has taken the Internet by storm. It has captured the hearts of mainstream computer users like no other Internet resource - and for good reason.

The Web allows even the most computer illiterate user to access the mind-numbing expanse of information available online - and it does this using colourful graphics, sound, animation and even video!

In essence, the Web (or more accurately the Web browsers that navigate it) hides what was previously an unwieldy collection of commands and dreary text-based menus. Web browsers display the Internet via a graphical-user-interface ("GUI", pronounced "gooey") that is both simple and intuitive to use.

At the click of a mouse button or the touch of a key, users can criss-cross the global information maze without requiring any technical understanding of how, where, why or by whom the connections are being made.

Click on a highlighted word or phrase in one document (a "hyperlink"), and you might find yourself viewing a related document downloaded from a computer on the other side of the globe. Once you are in the Web browser's GUI environment, you can move from area to area, document to document, and Web site to Web site at the click of a mouse button.

Since its humble beginning as a tool developed to help research scientists disseminate documents quickly and easily, the Web has evolved to cover a wide variety of uses.

You can order groceries, holidays and numerous other consumer goods online. Of

> **Tip**
> There are a number of excellent tutorials available online dealing with Search Engines and finding information. Have a look at this one: http://www.imagescape.com/helpweb/www/seek.html

more interest to readers of this book, you can also browse vast libraries of regularly updated information complete with photos, video and audio (a living encyclopedia, for want of a better description). We will look at this research aspect in later chapters.

Hypertext

The power of the Web lies in the concept of *hypertext*.

Hypertext is the name given to the process of displaying or arranging text on a computer screen in a manner that emulates human thought processes.

In a printed book, users must read sequentially through the text or manually skip through the pages and paragraphs (usually with the aid of an index or table of contents) in an attempt to locate information of specific interest to them.

The same usually applies when information is displayed in electronic form - users must page (or scroll) through the information to locate sections of relevance or interest.

The human brain, however, isn't always at its most efficient when it receives information in a sequential or linear manner.

For instance, you might be reading a passage of text when a word or concept catches your attention. You could continue reading through the text, waiting patiently until the concept is developed later on. But it is more likely that you will move on and read the connected passage, before eventually returning to where you left off.

Hypertext software allows information to be arranged and accessed in a manner similar to this. Hypertext documents are associative, not linear. This is achieved by incorporating links within the text that enable users to easily jump to another part of the document (or another document) containing related information and then return to where they left off.

On the Web, keywords are *linked* to other passages or documents. These keywords are generally displayed on screen in a different colour, *italicised* or underlined, allowing them to be readily identified. By moving the cursor or mouse pointer to that highlighted keyword and clicking, readers are taken to the related information.

Viewing documents on the Web

A Web browser is simply a software application that can interpret the links embedded in online documents and access these documents on demand.

On plain hypertext systems, all linked documents are usually on the same computer. But when this software has access to the connectivity of the Internet, it brings into play a whole new realm of information retrieval.

> **TIP**
> Web browsers are not limited to displaying documents. A link can contain commands instructing the browser to make ftp connections (to download software) or even link users to Usenet groups so that they can read newsgroups.

As mentioned earlier, Web documents can contain links that automatically connect the user to other documents anywhere on the Internet, even on the other side of the world.

You might be logged into an Australian university library via the Internet reading a document about *The Endeavour*. A reference to Captain James Cook is highlighted, so you click on the highlighted keyword. The link might refer to a document stored on a machine at Cambridge University in the United Kingdom. Your Web browser, in accordance with instructions contained in the link, would automatically connect to the Cambridge University computer and retrieve the related document.

All of this happens seamlessly in the background. You are not required to know or understand the commands necessary to make the connection across the Atlantic, nor how to retrieve the file in question, download or view it. Those commands are preconfigured into the document, and are acted upon by the Web browser.

As you can imagine, this represents a powerful tool for accessing information, allowing even the most computer illiterate users to make full use of the Internet.

Accessing the Web

Like most Internet resources, the Web is based on the client/server concept. Client software (Web browsers) connect to Web servers, which then pass on the information or documents requested.

Today, there are literally tens of thousands of Web servers around the world, containing hundreds of thousands of gigabytes of information, software and graphics. As the Web grows in popularity, more Web servers are including links to other servers around the world, allowing users to jump from server to server across the Internet.

What is the Web?

There are also a growing number of Web servers - known as Search Engines - dedicated to helping users search information available on the Web. We examine these in detail later in the book.

As with all Internet resources, how you use the Web depends upon the software you are running to access it.

If you are using a Web client, such as Netscape Navigator or Internet Explorer, refer to the online help reference that comes with the software. Alternately, there are a number of detailed reference guides available at most major bookshops. Failing this, you can always get detailed help from any of the FAQ files that cover Web browsers or the Web-specific newsgroups (we discuss these in detail later in the book).

What's a URL?

You will notice the term "URL" is often used when discussing Web browsing. URL is an acronym for *Universal Resource Locator*. Every document or service available on the Web has a URL. URLs are simply a standardised shorthand method of referring to resources available on the Internet (in essence, an "address" for that resource). Web browsers interpret these URLs when you instruct them to retrieve documents and so on.

For example, a hypertext document called mytext.html, stored on a computer called www.example.co.uk in the /pub/www directory, would have a URL of

www.example.co.uk/pub/www/mytext.html

All the information is the same as that set out longhand in the paragraph above. However, it is recorded in a specific order: machine first; then directory; then document name. This tells the Web browser all it needs to know to connect to the specified computer and call up the document.

A URL must be used in conjunction with one of several commands, such as the *http://* command.

http is an acronym for *hypertext transfer protocol*, which is the protocol defining how information is to be sent or retrieved via the Web. The **http://** command tells the browser that it should

> **Tip**
>
> Search Engines regularly update and modify their search functions in order to meet the increasing demands of users. It pays, then, to keep an eye on online tutorials to make sure that your knowledge is also up-to-date. Learn a little at http://www.windweaver.com/searchguide.htm

expect the document specified in the URL to be in hypertext (or Web) format and that it should act accordingly.

Specifying a URL

Most Web browsers have a "hot key" combination which activates a pop-up window, into which you type the URL of the Web site or resource you wish to visit.

As mentioned above, URLs must be specified in conjunction with a command that tells the browser the type of resource you want to access.

For example, to connect to a World Wide Web server and access a hypertext document (with a URL of www.net-works.co.uk/books.htm) using the Internet Explorer Web browser, type **<ctrl-o>** (the "hot key") and in the pop-up dialogue box type:

http://www.net-works.co.uk/books.htm

Understanding the Web

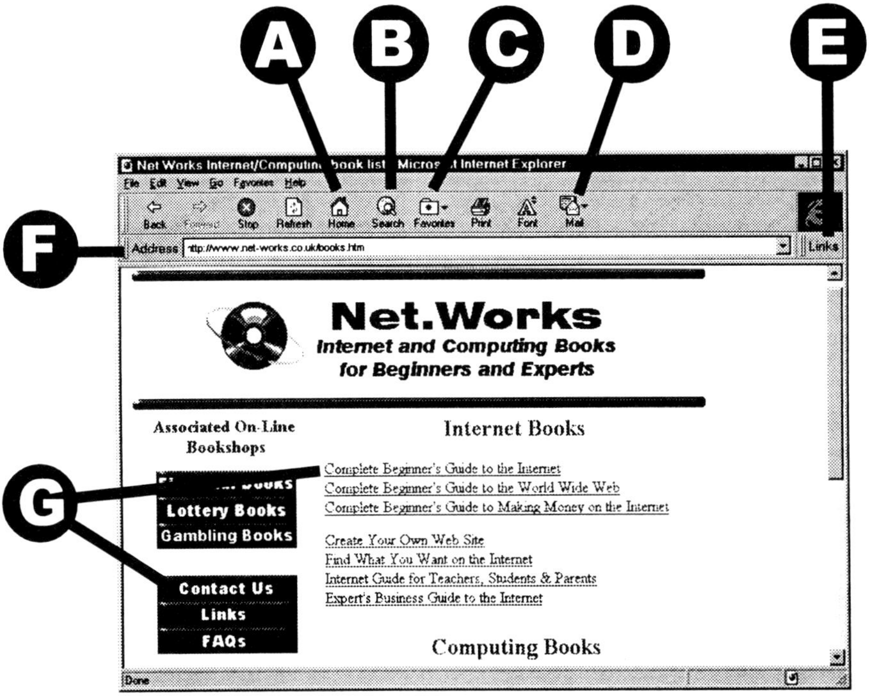

What is the Web?

(A) The 'home page' is where you start every Internet session.

(B) Click here to access a 'search engine'—a special Internet site which can find Web pages containing key words or phrases.

(C) When you discover an interesting Web site, add it to your Favourites folder so you can visit it again just by clicking this menu.

(D) Click here to send electronic mail (email) across the Net.

(E) Microsoft Internet Explorer lets you add single-click links to the sites you visit most often.

(F) This is the 'URL' or address of the current Web page.

(G) Click these 'hypertext' links to visit other pages on this Web site, or other sites anywhere around the world.

Conclusion

You should now be familiar with the basic operation of the Web, and concepts such as hypertext and URLs. In the following chapters we will examine principles of online information retrieval, as well as highlight skills that you will develop as you become more proficient at finding information online.

Chapter 2

The Virtual Library

Whether you are researching a project, preparing a class assignment, keeping abreast of your favourite hobby, checking your team's score in the latest game, looking for suitable holiday destinations or simply indulging in some recreational reading, you simply cannot beat the World Wide Web—both in terms of content and accessibility.

It's all there.

Regardless of your topic of interest, you will almost certainly find an information resource dedicated to it online.

Thanks to the growing acceptance of the Internet as a communications medium, a great deal of time, money and effort is being invested in its development. Governments, universities, schools, companies, community groups, clubs and even individuals are creating new online information resources.

The Internet offers access to magazines, books, articles, research, newspapers, newsletters and discussion papers covering the broad spectrum of human knowledge.

Formerly paper-bound government reports, court decisions, parliamentary records and national archives have been given a new lease of life - and a much larger audience - by being added to the wealth of online information.

There is now no need to wait for the next imprint of your favourite encyclopedia to find in-depth, expert discussions of current events and discoveries. Similarly, you no longer need rely on your daily paper

> *Tip*
> Not too sure which is the best place to start your searches? Well, then, it's back to school for you!
> http://www.classroom.net/classroom/searchingfaq.html

alone to provide coverage of community, national and international events that interest you.

During the trials of O.J. Simpson and Louise Woodward in the United States, interested online spectators could access up-to-the-minute court transcripts of evidence given by witnesses, as well as lawyers' statements.

The Atlanta Olympics was not only beamed into the lounge rooms of millions of couch potatoes, but also onto the computer screens of millions of Internet users. If your favourite Olympic event was not covered by TV or radio broadcasts, you could still follow the action via the official Web site.

If you are worried the Australians will make a mess of things in the 2000 Olympics, you can check on the activities of the Sydney Organising Committee for the Olympic Games at:

http://www.sydney.olympic.org.au/

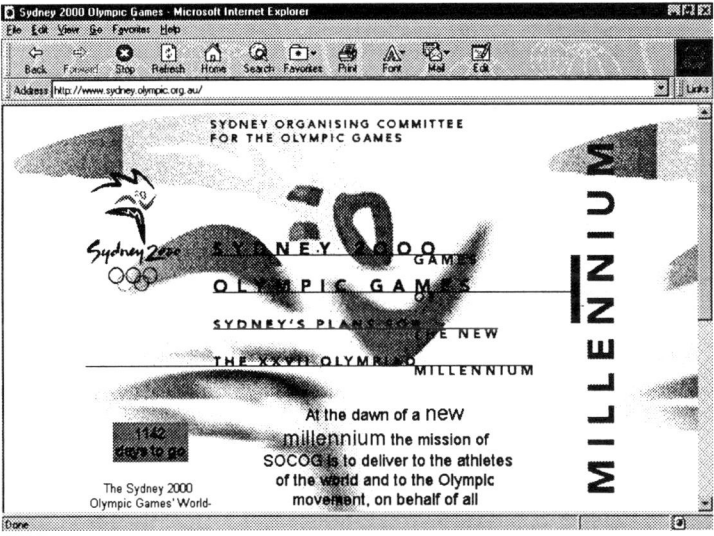

Or, if science is more your speed, take a look at the wealth of information resources on the Web.

At one time, researchers considered the local library to be *the* authoritative source of information, but now the Internet is regarded by many as the first port-of-call in research endeavours.

Lots of universities and research institutes publish data and papers online. Student essays and theses, previously stored away in archive boxes, are becoming available online. There are now entire catalogues of information, archival material, public records and the like to which public access was - even as recently as five years ago - inconceivable. This was not because governments and libraries wanted to lock this information away, but because there was no cost-efficient means of providing decentralised access to it.

The increasing cost of traditional paper-based distribution has convinced universities, governments and businesses to invest in electronic publishing services. Researchers and Internet users alike will benefit as the barriers restricting access to information are gradually dismantled.

Behind the hype

As any experienced Internet user will tell you, turning to the Internet for help is by no means as easy as looking in the reference section of your library for an encyclopedia.

The Internet's wealth of information is both a blessing and a burden.

Unlike resources in a library, information on the Internet is not clearly classified or categorised. You cannot, for instance, click on an icon marked *Botany* and have your Web browser display all Web sites containing information on plants. There is no online equivalent to the reference section, the newspaper reading area, or even the Dewey decimal system.

Any information you could want is out there, but it is spread across hundreds of thousands of computers, which act as hosts for the millions of pages of online information. Without a central index or cross-referencing system, how is it possible to track down a desired piece of information?

The key

The key to harnessing the information resources of the Internet, and in particular the Web, is knowing where to look.

This is not as trivial a skill as you might think.

With hundreds of thousands of computer hosts on the Internet, choosing the right starting point can make the difference between a fast, efficient search and one that is laborious and drawn-out. In some

The Virtual Library 17

cases, it might also mean the difference between a successful search and a fruitless one.

In the chapters that follow, we will examine some of the skills that make finding information online simpler and more intuitive. We'll also take a look at Web Search Engines and how they work. Understanding the inner mechanics of Search Engines will help you to use the search techniques discussed more efficiently.

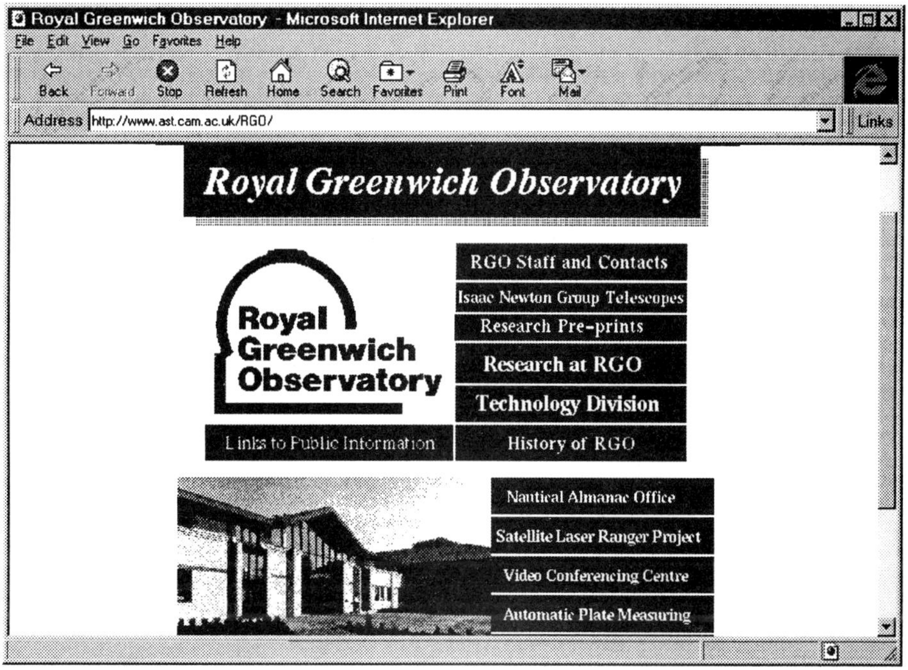

The Royal Greenwich Observatory is one of the many thousands of science sites to be found on the web. Take a look at:

www.ast.cam.ac.uk/RGO/

Chapter 3

The Information Chase

As children, we were taught basic information-finding skills. We all know, for instance, that libraries are an excellent resource for both fiction and non-fiction material, as are newspapers, magazines, video and film documentaries. We were taught how to use library card catalogues, how to search through footnotes and bibliographies for further references, and how to trace the evolution of a school of thought.

We were also taught that librarians, who possess an often-bewildering knowledge of the volumes that line the shelves, are there to help us. It's unlikely that many of us actually appreciate the services offered by librarians until we have to research a topic *without* their assistance.

The librarian's desk is, for many, the first point of contact in a library.

If you are looking for a specific book or author, the librarian can usually point you to the right section, sometimes even the right shelf.

A librarian's most useful role, however, is helping to narrow the scope of your research.

You may, for instance, be looking for information on dinosaurs. If you ask the librarian for help, s/he will first ask for more specific information on your search. Using this, the librarian can ascertain the nature of the material you are looking for - for instance, whether it is archaeological or anatomical - and point you in the right direction.

The burgeoning web

Web Search Engines can be seen as cyberspace "librarians".

Users submit a query, which the Search Engine uses to locate relevant sites. The Search Engine then displays details of matched sites for users to browse through and explore.

But here the similarity ends.

While Search Engines are central in helping users find their way around the Internet, they do have certain limitations.

Their massive databases of Web sites, coupled with high-end computers, allow users to find sites very quickly. But speed isn't everything. Search engines are as capable - and some would say as likely - to provide misdirections with equally blinding speed.

There are two major causes of difficulty, each of which aggravates the other.

The first problem is that few people (Internet users or otherwise) are trained in the "art" of locating information. There is more to research than simply collecting all the information available on a specific topic. Research requires planning - the more meticulous, the better.

The second problem is that online search tools, such as Search Engines, lack "intelligence". By asking a few pertinent questions a librarian can ascertain your true research goal, while a Search Engine will simply accept the information provided and display all matches in its database. The outcome is often search results comprised of a hotchpotch of relevant and irrelevant links.

The solution to this problem is two-fold.

Firstly, Internet users need to learn search skills which will enable them to narrow their field(s) of enquiry. Secondly, they should know how Search Engines work - especially more advanced search options, which can filter out irrelevant information. This book aims to instruct you in both these skills.

> **TIP**
> Search Engine Rule of Thumb: Every minute you spend considering and planning your search terms will probably save hours of wading through useless, unrelated links and Web sites.

Search strategies

A number of strategies can be used to make your Internet searches more fruitful and efficient. Several of these are discussed below.

Simple searches

The easiest way to search the Internet is using simple searches. To do this, connect to your favourite Search Engine, type your query in the text box and click on the search icon. It's fast, simple and requires little preparation.

> **TIP**
> If you are new to Search Engines, performing a few simple searches can help you get a feel for the way in which they work.

But it's also the type of search most likely to waste your time - since it will turn up hundreds, perhaps thousands, of irrelevant links and matches. As far as possible, avoid these types of searches.

Having said that, simple searches do play a minor role in the search process. Simple searches can introduce users new to Search Engines to the searching process.

At the same time, however, simple searches will show you just how much *stuff* is on the Web - convincing you of the need to use more specific searches.

Finally, the results of simple searches can help structure your search to provide the best results.

For example, I recently wanted to locate someone online (preferably in Britain) who could value a 1906 one penny coin that I found among some old knick-knacks. For the life of me, I couldn't think of the technical name for coin collecting (which is, by the way, numismatics, which means "of coins or coinage").

So, I connected to a Search Engine and used *coins* as a search term. There were 17,072 matches, ranging from vendors of coin purses to shareware finance programs. In the first few pages of links I found a reference to *coin collectors*, which was more specific than the search query I had used. I therefore used this as my search term in another simple search, which returned 1,304 matches. Scrolling through the listed sites, I soon located several which interested me.

Plan your search terms

Once you have performed a few simple searches, you will be convinced of the need to be more selective in your choice of **keywords**.

Wherever possible, choose specific terms over general terms. For instance, the keyword *yacht* is preferable to *boat*, and *chlorine* will produce more useful results than *chemical*.

When selecting appropriate keywords, consider how other users might categorise the information for which you are looking. Be aware of:

- **Spelling:** Some words can be correctly spelt in a number of different ways, such as *grey* and *gray*. Note the variations between British English and American English, such as *center* and *centre*, *favourite* and *favorite*, *colour* and *color*. This is particularly important given that almost three-quarters of Web-based information is of US origin.

- **Synonyms:** Use synonyms within your search query, either by expressly including or excluding them through the use of operators (described below). For instance, where we use the words *"car"* or *"motor vehicle"*, North Americans use *"automobile"*.

    For example, to find information on car paint, you might use a search query such as *paint AND (car OR automobile OR motor vehicle)*. By the way, this is also an example of the use of operators, which leads us to…

TIP

Sometimes using fewer search terms can be more productive. Too many search terms can lead to the Search Engine choosing the wrong term(s) as central to your search, "skewing" the results.

Get to know your operators

Almost all Search Engines support the use of **operators**. These are special words or symbols which, when included in your search query, give the Search Engine precise instructions on how to match Web sites to your query. This reduces the list of potential matches, while increasing the likelihood that the matched sites will be relevant to your search. Operators are examined in more detail a little later.

Are operators infallible? Unfortunately, no.

While operators allow users to specify the information they are looking for with greater accuracy, they do not remove all the ambiguity in the search process.

Very few Search Engines are developed using the expertise of a team of librarians or other research specialists. As a result, the information they gather is often categorised in a haphazard fashion. Even if your search query is precise, imperfect indexing or cataloguing on the Search Engine's part will affect the accuracy of your search results.

TIP

There is as yet no uniform Internet search "language". Each Search Engine varies vis-à-vis which operators it supports and how it uses them. To determine which operators are supported, visit the Search Engine's online help pages. These are generally written in simple, easy-to-understand language with plenty of examples.

Incremental searches

Many Search Engines support incremental searches, which allow you to progressively narrow down the results of your query by refining your search term(s).

For example, you might be concerned over the waiting lists present in the National Health System and be considering private health care.

> **TIP**
> Seasoned Web researchers swear by the practice of starting with specific searches, then moving to more general search terms if unsuccessful. This is only useful if you can narrowly define your goal at the outset.

Your first step could be to connect to a Search Engine and simply use *healthcare* as your search query. The number of *hits* (that is, matches to your search query) that are displayed will depend on which Search Engine you use: for instance, at the time of writing AltaVista returned 116,204 matches, whereas Yahoo! returned only 2096!

A quick look at the listings reveals that most of the sites, although covering the topic of "healthcare", are irrelevant to our search, because they relate to the US healthcare system.

So, how can we narrow down the results?

The answer is simple: use both *healthcare* and *uk* as the search query by typing *healthcare +uk* into the text box (note that there is a space **before** the + sign but not after it.)

If you try this yourself, you'll notice the search results are still quite broad. The Search Engines have matched every British web site which has anything to do with healthcare. AltaVista still shows 91 sites, but we are certainly closer to our goal.

Let's try another refinement of the search, by adding the term *private* type in *private +healthcare +uk*.

This brings us almost to our goal. Yahoo! finds fewer matches, and AltaVista's results are more focused.

Performing incremental searches, such as in the example above, can modify search terms to include and exclude specific search criteria, ensuring that only relevant sites are matched.

> **TIP**
> Be careful with synonyms. If your search involves several primary search terms, do not introduce synonyms unless you include them for all the terms. Otherwise the Search Engine could respond to the inclusion of synonyms by giving them (and the related primary search term(s)) more "weight", which will affect the overall accuracy of the search.

Partial searches

If you want to perform a general search, or are unsure of the best search terms to use, try your luck with a partial search.

When you perform a partial search, Search Engines will look for parts of words (known as **substrings**) which match your search term.

For instance, if you use the term *medic**, a partial search will turn up matches to words such as *medical, medicine, medicate, medicare* and so on. From the list of matched terms and sites you can decide which terms to follow up.

Boolean searches

Most Search Engines accept search queries that use Boolean operators. These include the words AND, OR, NOT and NEAR, as well symbols such as quotation marks and parentheses.

These terms are extremely effective filters of which sites should and should not be matched to your search query.

- **AND**

The AND operator instructs the Search Engine to only display documents or Web sites that contain *all* terms joined by the AND operator.

For example, to find only those documents and Web sites that contain the words *jurassic, park,* and *movie,* use: **jurassic AND park AND movie**.

Note: Some Search Engines allow you to swap AND with +.

- **OR**

The OR operator instructs the Search Engine to only display documents or Web sites that contain *at least one* of the words joined by the OR operator.

For example, to locate documents or Web pages that refer to Microsoft and/or Netscape, use: microsoft OR netscape

- **NOT**

The NOT operator instructs the Search Engine to ignore any page containing the word that appears after the NOT operator, even though it might have matched the other search queries.

For example, to find Web sites or documents that discuss pet care, but do not relate to cats, use: **pet AND care NOT cats**

Note: Some Search Engines require that NOT be used in conjunction with the AND operator, so that the above example would read: **pet AND care AND NOT cats**

Also, some Search Engines allow you to swap NOT with "-" (a negative sign).

- **( )**

Parentheses are used in more complicated searches to group portions of Boolean queries.

For example, to find cake recipes that use either bananas or apples, use: fruit AND recipes AND (banana OR apple)

- **" "**

Quotation marks tell a Search Engine to match only documents and Web sites that contain the search terms or phrases in the *order in which they are entered*.

For example, to search for Web sites that discuss The Millenium Bug (only), use: "the millenium bug".

> ## TIP
> Beware the default search format! Different Search Engines treat simple search queries differently. For example, some Search Engines use OR searches by default (that is, they match Web sites that contain any of your specified search terms) whereas others use AND searches (which only match sites if they contain all of your keywords).

Conclusion

You should now have a basic understanding of search strategies that can help to locate specific information. In addition, you should know how to use Boolean operators to initiate more accurate searches.

The next chapter will look at how Search Engines work, and following chapters will focus on popular Search Engines.

Chapter 4

The Anatomy of a Search Engine

When the World Wide Web first appeared on the Internet, only a handful of Web sites were publicly available. Users therefore memorised address details, or kept a list of available sites.

Soon, however, the number of Web sites grew, and within a year a hundred or so dotted the electronic landscape. Memorising all of these addresses was out of the question, so personal lists of sites became necessary. There was as yet no centralised list of new sites, so friends and colleagues would meet regularly (or email one another) with details of sites they had found.

Eventually, a few dedicated individuals created Web sites comprised purely of links to other sites. Yahoo!, one of the best known and highly regarded Search Engines, was created in 1994 by two University students, David Filo and Jerry Yang, for the sole purpose of keeping track of their favourite Web sites.

These first "**directories**" were fairly unsophisticated and rarely used any form of methodical organisation. However, as they increased in popularity, Web-based directories took on a life of their own. They soon became better organised - usually indexed alphabetically but occasionally divided into broad topics.

These directories helped Web users to find sites of interest, and this in turn stimulated interest in the Web as an information resource.

> **TIP**
> The Web is in a constant state of flux and sites reorganise their materials regularly. There is no guarantee that any of the matched sites or documents will still exist when you try to visit them! If you get an error message, try shortening the URL (by removing the last directory segment or by simply entering the domain name of the site) and then navigate through this site to see if the matched document still exists on it.

In the last few years, the number of Web sites on the Internet has skyrocketed. Although it is impossible to accurately survey the number of sites is certainly more than 500,000. Hundreds of new sites are being added *each day*.

This enormous expansion has made keeping track of what is available on the Web an inhuman task.

Enter the Search Engine.

Some users regard Search Engines as massive, **indexed** lists of Web sites and information resources, while others see them as huge databases containing information on just about every Web site available.

In fact, most Search Engines play the dual roles of Web site directory and searchable database of sites.

Search Engines employ special search programs - generically referred to as *spiders* or *web robots* - to make the tasks of indexing and categorising this wealth of information more manageable.

These programs traverse the Internet in search of new Web sites on behalf of a specific Search Engine. When they find one, they download all the information it contains, and then carefully examine this information to extract keywords and terms that can be used to index and categorise the site and its content.

These keywords are then added to the Search Engine's database, together with the address details and a description of the newly indexed site.

Spiders roam the Web continually, ensuring that the Search Engines controlling them have the most up-to-date information available.

TIP

A Search Engine does not actually search the Web for sites that match your query—the search process would simply take too long. Instead, the Search Engine scans its database of already indexed sites for matches. This enables it to provide you with a list of results in seconds, rather than days or weeks!

The role of Search Engines

There are essentially three types of Search Engines.

Passive Search Engines do not use spiders or similar programs. Instead, they rely on Internet users to submit details of their own or favourite Web sites. The submissions are added to the Search Engine's database for future reference.

Active Search Engines, on the other hand, rely on spider programs to maintain

The Anatomy of a Search Engine

and update their listings. They may also allow individuals to submit details of Web sites for inclusion; in this case, the details are either entered directly into the Search Engine's database or passed on to a spider program for investigation.

Finally, there are **Meta-Search** Search Engines. These are not Search Engines as such, but Web sites that can be used to search several Search Engines at the same time.

> *TIP*
> The order in which you specify your search terms is important to some Search Engines. Make it a habit to specify the most important terms first, regardless of which Search Engine you use.

Using Search Engines

There are generally two ways in which you can use a Search Engine: searching and browsing.

Searching

Most Search Engines provide a simple *search* or *query* function that can be used to locate Web sites or information of interest.

In essence, you simply type one or more keywords into a text box, and click on the search icon. The Search Engine then checks its extensive database for Web sites that match your keywords (referred to as "**hits**"), and it displays these in a list.

The list of hits will generally include the name of the Web site, its address (or URL) and a brief description of its content.

To visit a specific site, simply click on its name - which is displayed as a hyperlink - and your Web browser will open that site.

Once a Search Engine has received your search query, it can generally search its database (which might contain tens of millions of records) and display the results in a matter of seconds. How's that for service?

Browsing

You may prefer to use your Search Engine to browse - casually wandering through a *directory* listing of sites.

Browsing will take you from general headings (such as *Internet, Computers, Art, Science* and *Sport)* to very specific titles (such as *X-Rays, Internet Chat Software*, and *Heptathlon)*.

A Search Engine's main Web page usually contains a list of browseable headings that provide a breakdown of the sites it has indexed. Selecting the most appropriate heading for your search will lead to a page containing more specific sub-headings, which in turn lead to sub-sub-headings or sites.

If there isn't a heading specific to your topic, choose one that is related to it. For example, if you are looking for information on a particular type of dinosaur, select *Science* as your general heading, and then navigate through the sub-headings until you find one relevant to dinosaurs.

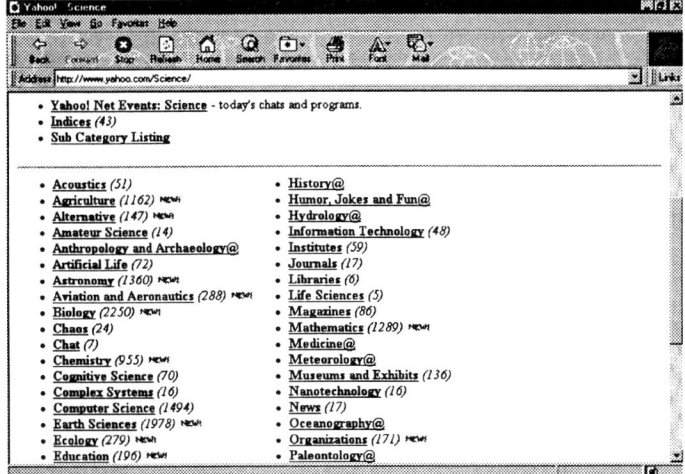

The Yahoo! Search Engine displays numerous sub-categories under the Science heading

For instance, from the list of sub-categories displayed above, you can select a heading that is closer to your topic of interest - such as *paleontology*, the study of life in the geological past.

Selecting the paleontology sub-heading displays a list of sub-sub-headings, as well as a list of specific sites

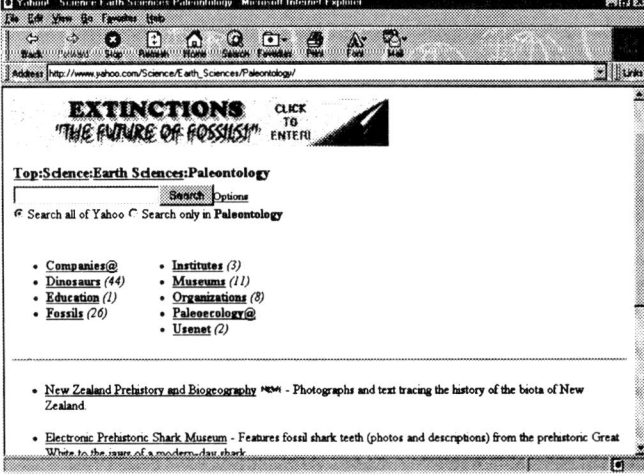

The Anatomy of a Search Engine

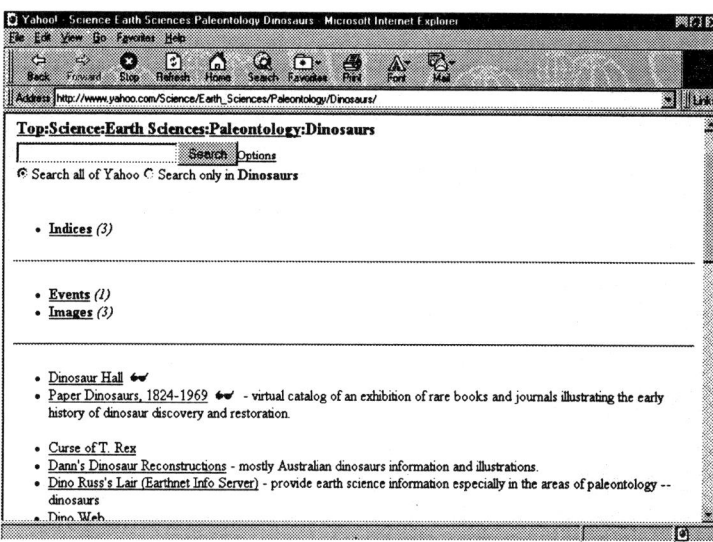

By clicking on the dinosaur sub-sub-heading, we can call up a list of sites and their descriptions. Browsing through these allows us to determine which sites best suit our needs

Conclusion

By now you should know that there are three major types of Search Engines: **Passive, Active** and **Meta**-Search Search Engines.

There are also two main methods of using Search Engines: keyword **searches** and **directory** browsing. Keyword searches are useful when you are searching for a specific subject (such as a particular species of dinosaur - say, *Tyrannosaurus Rex*), whereas directory browsing is suggested when you want general information on a topic.

Chapter 5

Information Retrieval Concepts

The Web is a librarian's nightmare, as its vast information resources are growing in a rapid, unstructured fashion. It can be likened to an encyclopedia in which the contents are not alphabetically ordered, and where entries may contain references to related materials.

To find information on the Web, therefore, it may appear your only option is to browse randomly until you find a site containing relevant material, or to ask friends or colleagues to point you in the right direction.

Both methods are commonly used by those unfamiliar with searching the Web. But there is a better way.

Current solutions

Search Engines can help you find information within the unstructured mass of the Web in several ways.

Yahoo! and Lycos, for instance, offer search functions, but rely more heavily on their hierarchical, structured categorisation of the millions of Web sites they index. These types of Search Engines act as a (incomplete) table of contents for the Web, and are preferred by users who like to browse indexes of sites.

Others, like AltaVista, Excite and HotBot place greater emphasis on their powerful search interfaces. These allow users to locate information and Web sites using keywords.

> **TIP**
> When you use a Search Engine for the first time, be sure to read its online help screen.

Information Retrieval Concepts

Although neither type of Search Engine represents a complete solution to the problems created by the unstructured, poorly-organised Web of information, they do at least make it easier to find what you want. Perhaps the next generation of Search Engines will close the gap.

> **TIP**
> If you do not find a relevant link within the first 10 to 30 matches, try searching again with a modified query.

Information quantity or quality

In the meantime, there is another, more vexing issue at hand - the quality of information available online.

The Internet, and the Web in particular, is the electronic equivalent of the Gutenberg press, in that it removes many of the barriers to producing and publishing information for the masses.

Almost anyone can create a Web site and publish what purports to be an authoritative exposition of a specific subject or topic. The normal safeguards found in other forms of publishing - editors, research boards and so on - are simply not in place.

As information consumers, we are generally trusting. Through our experience with the printed word we have come to associate printed material with authority; that is, if a publisher has deemed information suitable for print, we assume we can rely on its content.

Obviously, there are limits to such acceptance. If a printed pamphlet distributed by hand in the local mall contradicts everything we understand about a topic, we are unlikely to accept its assertions without secondary corroborating material.

Assessing the authority of sources or types of information is a skill acquired through years of experience. Few primary school children, for example, can measure the authoritative value of printed material. For this reason, their studies are restricted to school libraries, where the materials available have been selected on the basis of appropriateness and content.

> **TIP**
> With Search Engines, you get what you ask for—so to save hours of tedious trawling, it pays to learn how to construct useful search queries.

The research skills of secondary school students, however, enable them to select the "best source" of authoritative information. That is, when faced with material that deviates substantially from information given by known, reputable sources, they know to defer to the content of the most reputable source.

How well do these skills transfer to the Internet? Because of the nature of the Internet, it is very easy for individuals and organisations to clothe themselves in the garments of authority, while publishing what amounts to poorly researched information - or even worse, misinformation!

> **TIP**
> Most Search Engines ignore commonly occurring words, such as "a", "and", "the" and so on, so you needn't bother including these in your search queries.

Levels of authority

How, then, can you determine between authoritative and dubious information on the Internet? The guide below describes the types of information available on the Internet, and how each generally ranks in terms of authoritative content:

Established information sources

Many well-known reference sources, such as the *Encyclopædia Britannica*, and news and current affairs sources, such as *Time* magazine, *The Age* newspaper and *The New York Times,* have Web sites that provide access to information, special reports and so on.

Such sites can be assumed to be authoritative sources of information, in the absence of events that give rise to suspicion. By this, I mean that intuition still plays a role.

For instance, there have been a number of reports of computer vandals breaking into Web sites and posting obnoxious materials, such as nude photographs and so on.

If I were to connect to CNN's Web site - which would otherwise constitute an authoritative information source - and see a headline report that Martians had stopped by to visit Buckingham Palace, I would assume the story to be a hoax or a result of computer vandals, unless it was corroborated.

Secondary information sources

This category includes research findings, official reports and publications from such bodies as universities, government committees and "think tanks", as well as research papers prepared by lecturers, research students and the like.

Information Retrieval Concepts

Although each individual resource might differ in value and authority, collectively this group is reasonably authoritative. However, prudence dictates that some form of corroborating material be sought.

Individual and corporate sites

Numerous individuals and companies who are experts in their fields offer Internet users access to information and materials that are second-to-none in terms of authority.

However, it is difficult to distinguish these experts from the many Internet buffs who use the Web as a soapbox for airing their own views, beliefs, paranoia, conspiracy theories and general opinions on life and current events.

While individual sites can offer a wealth of credible information, it's generally best to look to other, more reliable sources of information (such as those in the categories above) before simply accepting the information and materials found on these sites.

Other research issues

There are other problems created by the use of Web sites for research. Two of the most important are copyright and attribution.

Many Internet users believe in the "information wants to be free" philosophy, and therefore don't think twice about "borrowing" material from books, magazines and even other sites to include in their sites. When material is quoted from traditional sources, it is quite straightforward to include the appropriate copyright information. But when information is published electronically, it is not as easy to verify ownership of information or its original source.

Similarly, attributing information found on the Web can be difficult. For instance, when quoting a passage from an essay in the *Harvard Business Review*, I use a standard format to attribute both the author and source. But how do I attribute a quote obtained from a Web site, a Usenet posting or personal email correspondence?

These are only some of the issues that remain to be resolved concerning the use of the Internet as a research source.

Chapter 6

Yahoo!

Yahoo! was one of the first Search Engines, and remains one of the most popular. It began its life as an online directory of favourite Web sites. Despite the transition to a multi-million dollar commercial venture, Yahoo! still retains much of the look, feel and structure it had in the early days.

One of Yahoo!'s prime strengths is the categorising of its content. As you can see from the screenshot below, much of the site's opening page is devoted to listing categories available for browsing.

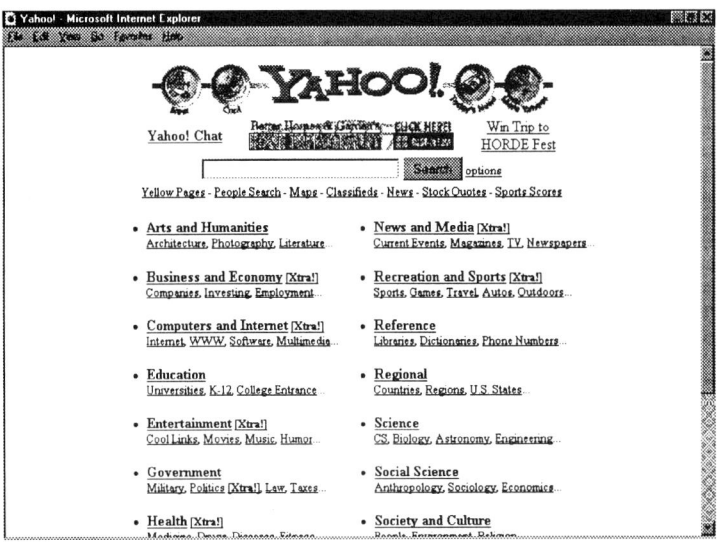

The Yahoo! Search Engine, located at http://www.yahoo.com

Yahoo! is the best port-of-call when you wish to perform a general search, rather than look for information on a particular topic. Although Yahoo! does offer a powerful search function, its strong points are its organisation and structure.

Perhaps Yahoo!'s true strength lies in the way in which it combines search features and category structure.

For example, you may be interested in motorcycles - not a specific motorcycle, such as a Ducati or Harley Davidson, but motorcycles in general. In the screenshot above, we can see that Yahoo! lists a category titled *Recreation and Sports*. Once this is selected, sub-categories will be shown, among which are *Sport* and *Autos*. Following either of these sub-category headings should eventually lead to a further sub-category related to motorcycles (either the sport of motor-cycle racing, or motorcycles themselves).

A quicker course of action would be to simply type *motorcycle* into the search box, click on the Search button, and allow Yahoo! to work its magic.

When you use Yahoo!'s search function, it retrieves and displays three kinds of information in the search results:

- All Yahoo! categories that match your search term(s).
- All Web sites in its database that match your search term(s).
- The Yahoo! categories listing the matched Web sites.

This breakdown provides an excellent platform for further research. Users can either drill down into Yahoo!'s category headings by following the matched category headings, or jump directly to any of the matched sites via hyperlinks which are displayed in the search results.

To continue with our earlier example, if we were to use *motorcycle* as our search term, Yahoo! would find a number of matches:

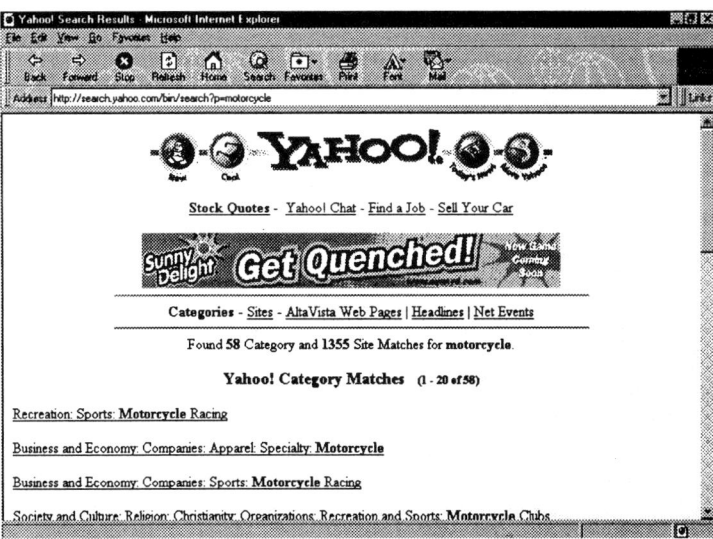

The results of our 'motorcycle' search using Yahoo!

In fact, it found 58 category and 1355 site matches for *motorcycle*. Yahoo! therefore found a total 1413 hits, which it will display 20 at a time.

Results of Yahoo! searches provide two different types of information sources. Using the 58 directory headings (or categories) which relate to motorcycles, users who wish to can continue browsing, while the 1355 specific sites offer a wealth of information to those who want to jump directly to a Web site and begin gathering information.

Basic Yahoo! search tips

- Yahoo! is case insensitive; that is, it ignores capital letters.
- By default, Yahoo! searches its database for sites and categories which contain *all* your keywords. This can be modified using operators.

Advanced search options

Yahoo! offers a special search page (via the *options* link next to the Search button) for those who wish to use its advanced search features. These include the ability to search both Yahoo!'s listings and Usenet newsgroups for information, as well as to look for email addresses. Here you can also modify the number of matched categories or sites displayed per page, and restrict your search to new listings.

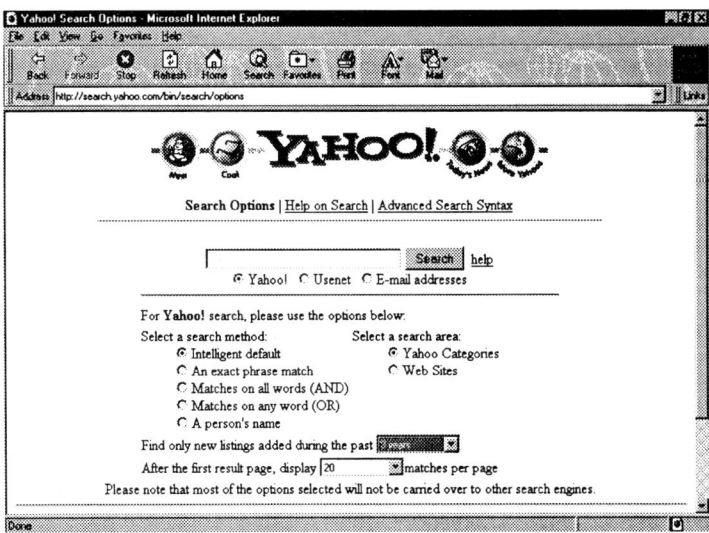

Yahoo!'s advanced search options at
http://www.yahoo.com/bin/search/options

Yahoo!

Advanced search syntax

- **Required words:** Attaching a + to a word instructs Yahoo! to find that word in all matches. For example, if you are looking for a fiery Indian recipe, use *indian +curry* rather than just *indian*.

- **Prohibited words:** Conversely, attaching a – to a word instructs Yahoo! to exclude any matches containing it. If you are looking for information about dinosaurs in the Jurassic era, but want to avoid links to sites reviewing a certain Spielberg movie, use the search term *jurassic –park*.

- **Document titles:** If you want to restrict Yahoo!'s searches to document titles only, use the **t:** option. For instance, to find documents which have titles containing the words *lung cancer*, use *t:lung cancer*. Document titles are the names given to individual Web pages by their creators. As such, they may or may not be an accurate guide to the document's contents.

- **URL limitations:** To instruct Yahoo! to search only for URLs containing your search term, use the **u:** option. For example, to find all URLs with Microsoft in them, use *u:microsoft* as your search query. This can be helpful if you are looking for the domain name of a company or organisation. For instance, if you did not know the domain name used by BP, you could use this search option to locate Web sites owned by BP.

- **Phrase matching:** If you want to find only exact matches for specific phrases, place the phrase in quotation marks. For example, to find an exact match for the phrase London Tower, use *"london tower"* as your search term.

- **Wildcard searches:** Yahoo! supports the use of wildcard searches, which are marked with an asterix (*). If you insert a wildcard to the right of a partial word, such as *gold**, it will find matches for all words beginning with gold, such as goldilocks and goldbrick.

Full details of Yahoo!'s advanced search syntax can be found at **http://search.yahoo.com/search/syntax?**

Chapter 7

AltaVista

AltaVista was a comparatively late entry into the world of Web Search Engines. Mind you, it has certainly made up for that since it hit the streets. It was originally designed to showcase a hardware/software combination developed by Digital Equipment Corporation, who own and maintain the site.

It went live on 15 December 1995, boasting a database containing the *full text* of over 16 million (yes, 16,000,000) pages of online information. Within six months, this database had grown to 30 million pages!

AltaVista claims to be one of the Internet's largest and fastest Web Search Engines - and it has some pretty impressive technology to back this claim. For example, Scooter - its custom designed Web robot - accesses around 3 million Web pages each day, passing on information to AltaVista's indexing software, which can process 1Gb of text per hour. All this makes AltaVista a pretty mean site - and an excellent research resource.

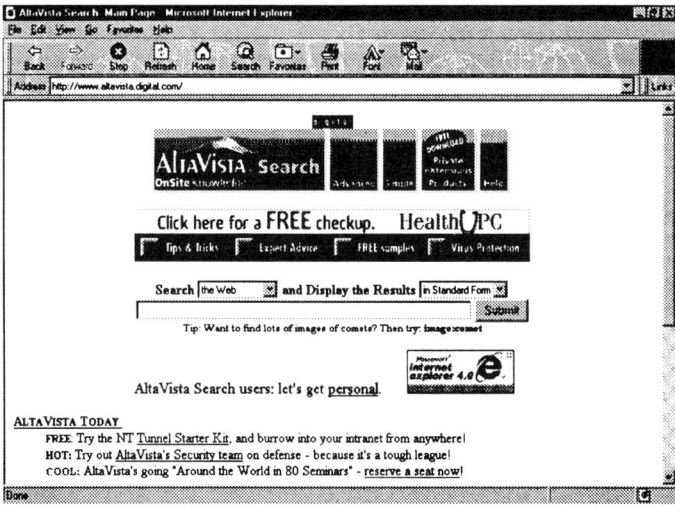

The main AltaVista Search Engine at http://www.altavista.digital.com

AltaVista

Searching with AltaVista

AltaVista is a Search Engine in the purest sense of the term, as it does not offer category browsing. Users simply type their search term(s) into the box provided, and click on *Submit*.

By default, AltaVista searches its database for each word used in the search query.

As AltaVista stores the full text of every Web site it has indexed, this often leads to many tens of thousands of matches, especially if your search query contains one or more general words. You can reduce this number by using more specific keywords and advanced searches, discussed below.

When displaying search results, AltaVista ranks Web sites that contain the largest number of matching words first. Sites that contain fewer matching words are ranked lower in the list. For example, the results of a search query using the keywords *British Rugby League* will list documents containing all three words before documents that only contain matches to two (say, *Rugby League)* or one (say, *Rugby)* of the words.

Basic searches

As mentioned earlier, by default AltaVista will search its database for each word in your search query, and list results in order of the highest number of matched words.

As part of its ranking process, AltaVista also gives priority to matched pages where:

- The search term(s) or phrase(s) is found in the title of the matched document.
- The search terms or phrases are located in close proximity to one another within the text of the matched document.
- The matched document contains more than one instance of the search term(s) or phrase(s).

Advanced searches

- **Default operator:** Unless special operators are included in a search query, AltaVista assumes the default operator is **OR**. If, for example, the search query is *motorcycle racing*, AltaVista will look for documents containing either *motorcycle* or *racing*, and display all hits.

- **Quotation marks:** To limit AltaVista's matches to sites which contain both or all of your search terms, place them within quotation marks. This instructs AltaVista to look only for exact matches to your query. For example, the search query "great barrier reef" will force AltaVista to only match documents containing that phrase.
- **Case sensitivity:** AltaVista is specifically case sensitive. If you specify *apple* as your search term, AltaVista will return matches for *apple*, *Apple* and *APPLE*. However, if you use *Apple* or *apPle*, AltaVista will only match *Apple* and *apPle* respectively.
- **Required words:** Attaching a + to a word instructs AltaVista to find that word in all matches. For example if you were looking for information regarding pink diamonds, use *diamond +pink* instead of just *diamond*.
- **Prohibited words:** Conversely, attaching a – to a word instructs AltaVista to exclude any matches containing that word. If you were looking for information on diamonds, but wanted to avoid information about our Argyle diamonds, try *diamond –argyle*.
- **Wildcard searches:** AltaVista supports the use of wildcard searches. If you insert a wildcard * to the right of a partial word (say, *hydro**), it will find matches for all words beginning with hydro (such as hydrocarbon, and hydrofoil).

    Wildcards can also be used to search for pages containing plurals of the search term(s), as well as to catch possible spelling variations (e.g. *alumi*m* will catch both the English (aluminium) and North American spelling (aluminum)).

Advanced search options

AltaVista offers an advanced search options page, accessed by clicking on the Advanced link on the main page.

Within this page, users can enter search terms containing Boolean logic, and elect to match either Web pages or Usenet postings. Users can also modify the ranking of hits (by specifying priority ranking terms), as well as exclude Web sites indexed before or after a specified date.

Special Web-related search options

AltaVista allows users to take full advantage of its database through the use of special operators. These include:

AltaVista

- **anchor:**free software

Matches Web sites that contain the specified word or phrase (in our example, *free software*) in the text of a hyperlink.

- **host:**net-works.co.uk

Matches Web pages with the phrase *net-works.co.uk* in the URL of the Web server.

- **link:**net-works.co.uk

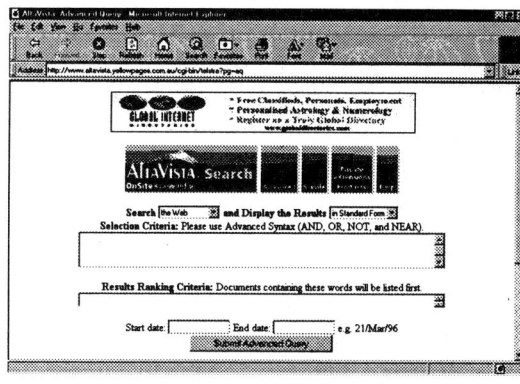

AltaVista's advanced search options page

Matches Web sites that contain at least one link to a Web site with *net-works.co.uk* in its URL.

- **text:**Beginner

Matches Web sites that contain the word *Beginner* in any part of the visible text of a page.

- **title:**"Spin Doctor"

Matches Web pages with the phrase *Spin Doctor* in the title. Don't forget, Alta Vista is case sensitive!

Live Topics

For Internet users who have Java-enabled Web browsers (which covers anyone using version 3 or above of Netscape or Internet Explorer), AltaVista offers a very handy service called *Live Topics*.

Essentially, AltaVista's Live Topics is a very intelligent search wizard. It analyses the contents of all the documents and Web sites that match your original query and then compiles a list of additional and associated search terms (i.e. keywords).

These associated terms are displayed in a list, or as a graphical depiction (depending on whether your browser supports Java). You then have the option of including or excluding these additional search terms from your original search query, and trying the search again. This allows you to narrow the focus of your searches.

Chapter 8

Excite

Excite looks and feels similar to other Search Engines that offer both browsing and search functions. In addition to a search box, it offers 14 "channels" for users to explore.

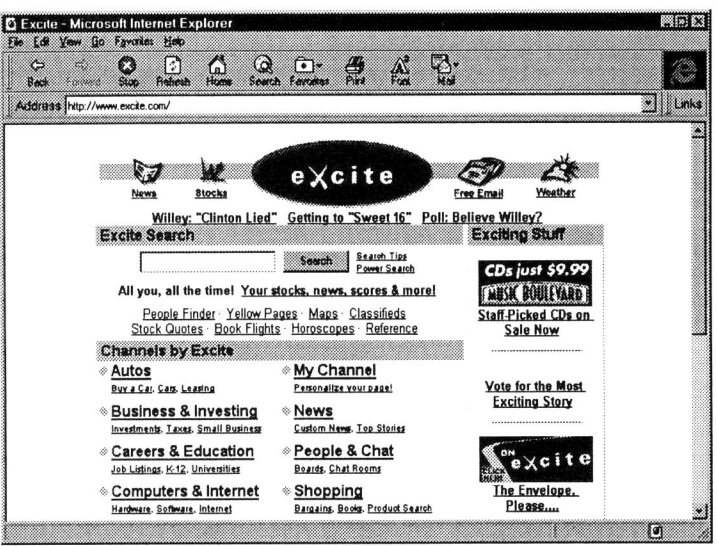

The Excite Search Engine located at http://www.excite.com

However, Excite claims to have the edge over other Search Engines with its ICE (Intelligent Concept Extraction) technology. Using this technology, Excite not only scans its databases for exact matches of your search term(s), but also attempts to find pages that are "conceptually" linked to your query.

For example, if you were to search for *confectionery*, Excite would realise that *chocolate* was a related topic, and also find matches for chocolate.

This aspect of Excite's search function makes it very useful for novice researchers, who might otherwise miss excellent Web resources as a result of improperly structured or narrow search criteria. Conversely, if you already know exactly what you want, it can turn up an annoying number of unrelated links.

Other services

In addition to general search services, Excite offers a number of useful resources for Internet researchers - including online classifieds, a people finder and email address lookup service.

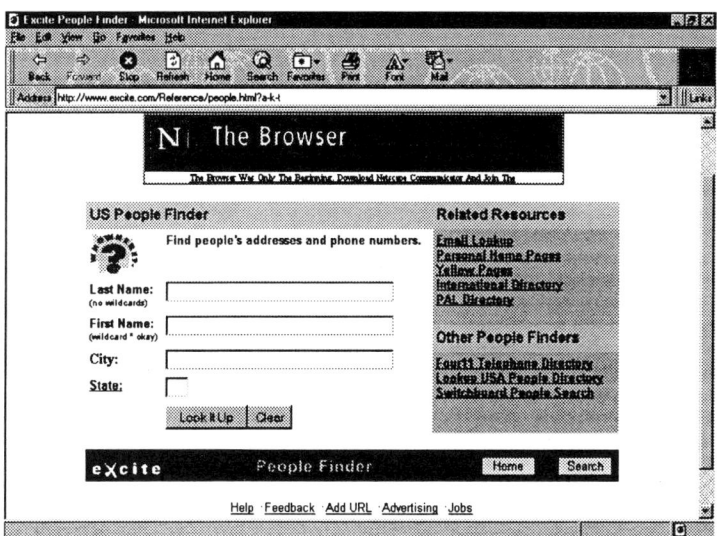

Finding a long lost friend is simple using Excite's people finder

Excite also offers a variety of US and international maps, as well as a US Yellow Pages service (unfortunately of little use to British users). These services can be accessed via links on Excite's main Web page. Map images can be printed or saved in graphic format for future reference.

Channel surfing

Excite has, currently, 14 'channels' available for browsing on its main Web page. Clicking on a channel calls up a detailed "channel guide", which contains links to related sub-channels, channel-related news and events, as well as other novelty items.

By following these links you will be transported from general topics to more specific areas and Web sites.

For instance, if you select the *Lifestyle* channel on the main Excite Web site, you will be provided with many related options and links, as shown in the screenshot below.

Selecting a sub-category (such as *Hobbies*) displays a list of further sub-channels and links to related Web sites, as shown below.

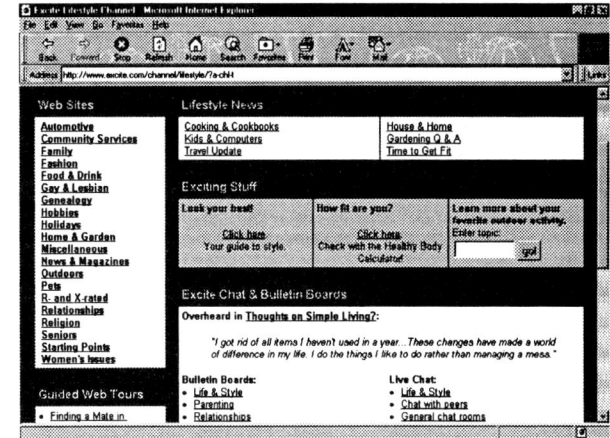

The Excite Lifestylechannel allows you to move from a general topic to more specific topics and Web sites

Basic searches

To perform a simple search using Excite, type your search term(s) into the text box on the main page and click on the *Search* button. Excite will search its database for Web sites that match both your search query and any related concepts.

- **Default operator:** The default operator is OR; that is, Excite will search for Web sites that contain any of the specified search terms. To limit Excite to a direct match of a phrase or several search terms, place them within quotation marks.

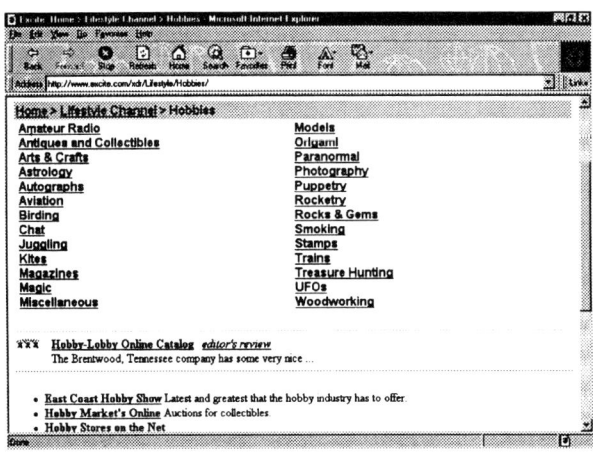

Selecting the sub-category Hobbies leads to a list of further sub-channels to choose from, as well as a collection of links to related Web sites

- **Search results:** Excite lists the matched hits in order of relevance to your search query. The more search terms a matched Web site contains, the higher it will appear in the list.

- **Required words:** Attaching a + (plus

sign) to a word instructs Excite to find that word in all matches. For example, if you were a fan of Mel Gibson, you would use *Mel +Gibson* to weed out unrelated links.

- **Prohibited words:** Conversely, attaching a − (minus sign) to a word instructs Excite to exclude any matches which contain that word. Continuing with the above example, to specifically exclude links to Mel Brooks, you might use *Mel +Gibson −Brooks*

Excite Boolean searches

If you use Boolean search operators (AND, OR, and NOT) as part of your search criteria, Excite will "switch off" its concept search capabilities and instead match only those sites which meet your search criteria.

Excite Power Search

Excite has a special Power Search menu, available via a hyperlink next to the *Search* button, which experienced searchers can use to control which sites are and are not included within their search parameters.

Using pull-down menus in the Power Search menu, users can elect to search the entire Web (but not Usenet), Web sites reviewed by Excite, or the databases of specific geographical versions of Excite, such as Excite France, UK or Sweden.

Additional text boxes allow users to specify in detail terms, words or phrases that should or should not be matched.

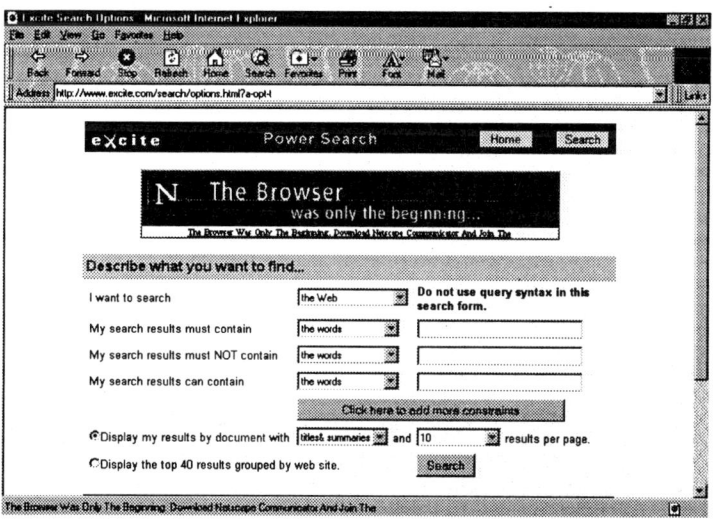

Chapter 9

HotBot

HotBot is another Search Engine originally designed to showcase new technology. It is built around NOW (Networks of Workstations) "clustering" technology, designed by Inktomi Corp.

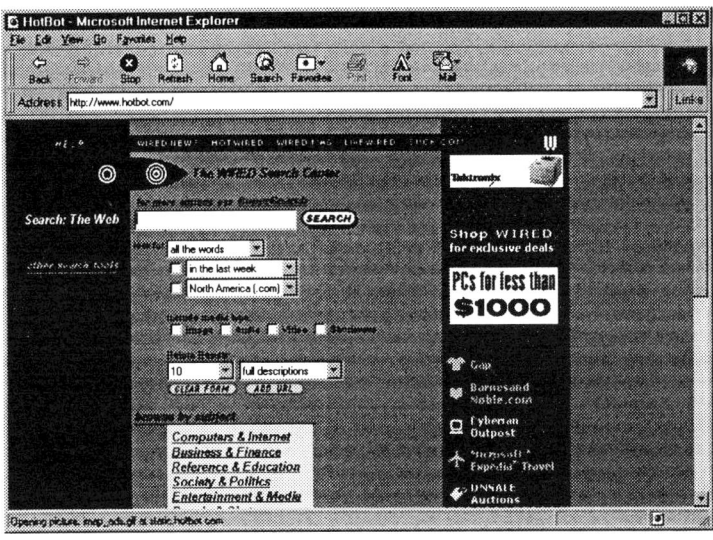

The HotBot Search Engine at http://www.hotbot.com

Instead of relying on a single, very fast high-powered (read "very expensive") computer to perform database searches, HotBot uses a network of smaller, cheaper computers (not unlike the one sitting on your desk at home or in the office) to scour its database on behalf of users.

These computers work together, sharing the workload of the Search Engine, and contributing processing speed and power to analysing user queries, searching HotBot's database and displaying results. One of the prime benefits of this technology is the ease with which processor power and speed can be added (simply hook up a few more computers) and the fact that failure of one or more computers will not unduly affect the overall service.

SmartCrawl

Despite this impressive hardware technology, the real magic behind HotBot is its Web spider software, *SmartCrawl*.

Standard Web spiders work by contacting a Web site, scanning its contents, selecting appropriate index terms, and then sending these details back to the Search Engine's database for processing and storage. SmartCrawl, on the other hand, handles all facets of the process - from crawling and searching to indexing - and automatically updates HotBot's database. Hosted by a clustered network of high-end Pentium Pro PCs, SmartCrawl is able to process 10 million pages of information each day!

Basic searches

HotBot offers search functions only, and does not cater for browsing.

To perform a search, type your search term(s) in the text box provided and click on the *Search* icon.

In addition to allowing users to enter search operators directly, HotBot allows users to modify various aspects of their search via pull-down menus.

By clicking on the pull-down menu, users can limit their search to either Web sites, Usenet articles, or search both the Web and Usenet. By default, HotBot will search the Web only.

The next pull-down menu provides easy access to HotBot's additional search functions:

- **All of the words:** Selecting this option will instruct HotBot to perform a search similar to one using the Boolean AND operator. HotBot will only search for Web sites containing all of the search terms, although not in any specific order.

- **Any of the words:** HotBot will perform a standard OR search; that is, it will look for Web sites which contain any of the search terms specified.

- **The exact phrase:** HotBot will search for Web sites that contain the search terms in the exact order specified. This is equivalent to entering your search terms in quotation marks.

- **The person:** This option instructs HotBot to look for near matches to your search query - useful when trying to locate a person's email address or personal Web site. For example, if you used *Mark Neely* as your search term, HotBot would return matches such as *Mark Neely*, *Mr M. Neely* and *Mark Felix Neely*.

- **Links to this URL:** Useful when you are trying to find Web sites that contain links to your own or a favourite Web site. It is also useful to see whether other users have included links on their Web pages to your Web site.
- **The Boolean expression:** Allows searchers to enter Boolean search queries directly.

> **TIP**
>
> Librarians are very savvy when it comes to finding information, be it in books or online. So it pays to listen to what they have to say. *Effective Use of Web Search Engines* sounds like a dry policy paper, but it is in fact a very handy guide to using Search Engines. Read it at http://www.state.wi.us/agencies/dpi/www/search.html

Super searches

HotBot sports several highly configurable advanced search menus. These allow users to limit HotBot's search results to, among other options, specific countries, Web sites or domain names, or Web resources created before or after a certain date.

To access these advanced options, click on either of the *Modify*, *Date*, *Location*, *Media Type* or *Page Type* icons (located down the left-hand side of the main page). When you click on an icon, the related menu options will be displayed.

To display all of the advanced search options at once, click on the *Open All* icon.

- **The Modify panel:** Use this panel to narrow the focus of your search by specifying additional search terms that must, should or should not be included in the matched documents.
- **The Date panel:** Use this panel to include or exclude documents or other resources which were created before, after or within a certain period. For example, if you are looking for news reports on a recent break-in at the Louvre, you could use Louvre as your search term, and limit matches to documents created around the date of the robbery.
- **The Location panel:** This allows you to limit your searches to a specific country or region (*GeoPlace*) or Web site or domain name (*CyberPlace*).
- **The Media Type panel:** You can limit HotBot's hits to Web sites which contain a certain media type (such as an audio file, image or

HotBot

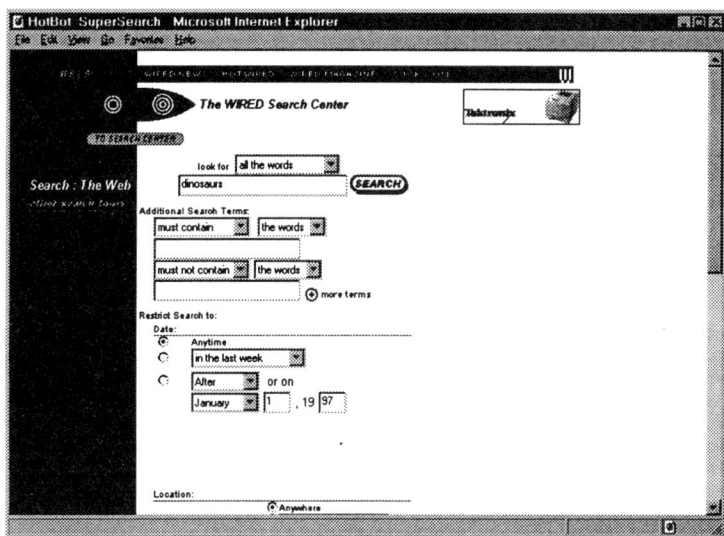

video). This is exceptionally useful for locating particular image or sound files for use in presentations, multimedia documents (or even your own Web site).

- **Page Type panel:** This limits how deep within a site HotBot will search to find a matching page or document. For example, think of a Web site as a flowchart. The main Web page is at the top of the flowchart. It might contain four links to other documents, which in turn contain three links each to further documents. The main Web page is the first level, the four documents linking from it constitute the second level, and the twelve documents linked from them constitute the third level. The closer your matched terms are found to the first level of documents, the more likely it is that the Web site will be relevant to your needs.

Chapter 10

WebCrawler

In a genesis shared by many early Web resources, a university student, Brian Pinkerton, created WebCrawler as a computer science project. It began as a small, single-user program designed to help Pinkerton find information on the Web. However, his classmates soon convinced him to make the tool available to other Internet users by integrating a Web site front-end.

WebCrawler's user-friendly interface can be found at http://www.webcrawler.com

The WebCrawler site first went live on 20 April 1994, containing information from around 6,000 Web sites, and running from the University's own network. It soon proved to be very popular. In fact, it became a little too popular—placing considerable strain on the University's limited computer resources. In early 1995, therefore, WebCrawler was sold to an American Internet Service Provider, America Online, and moved to a much larger, faster server. Excite Inc. (owner of the Excite Search Engine discussed earlier) now owns it.

WebCrawler

WebCrawler was one of the first full-text Search Engines available on the Internet, and it is still one of the most powerful. In recent years, its interface has been significantly modified, to make it easier - and more fun - to use.

Searching for beginners

In an effort to make WebCrawler easier to use, its owners have developed sophisticated computer algorithms that allow it to support "natural language searching". This means that Internet users no longer need to learn bothersome and confusing search syntax to obtain good search results. Instead, they merely type their search query in "plain English" into the text box provided, and then click on *Search*.

For example, if you were looking for a photograph of the Nile river, instead of *"Nile river" AND photo* users could simply type *photo of the Nile river*.

For those who are comfortable with operators and the like, WebCrawler also supports standard search syntax.

WebCrawler searches its database for Web sites which match any or all of your search terms; that is, it performs a standard OR search for Web sites containing at least one of your search terms, as well as looking for Web sites that contain all of them. Results are displayed with sites containing the most matched terms listed first.

Advanced searching

As mentioned earlier, although geared towards the novice user, WebCrawler does support a number of advanced operators that allow users to limit their search criteria; including:

- **AND:** Used to locate Web sites that contain two or more specified search terms (such as *fried AND eggs*).

- **OR:** Used to find Web sites that contain either or both of the specified words (such as *kangaroo OR wallaby*).

- **NOT:** Used to locate Web pages that contain the first word, except where they also include the second word (such as *science NOT fiction*).

- **ADJ:** Used when the search terms must appear adjacent to one another (such as *mark ADJ neely*).

WebCrawler Guides

If browsing is more your scene, WebGuide offers a directory service of 18 main Guides, some of which are shown in the screenshot below:

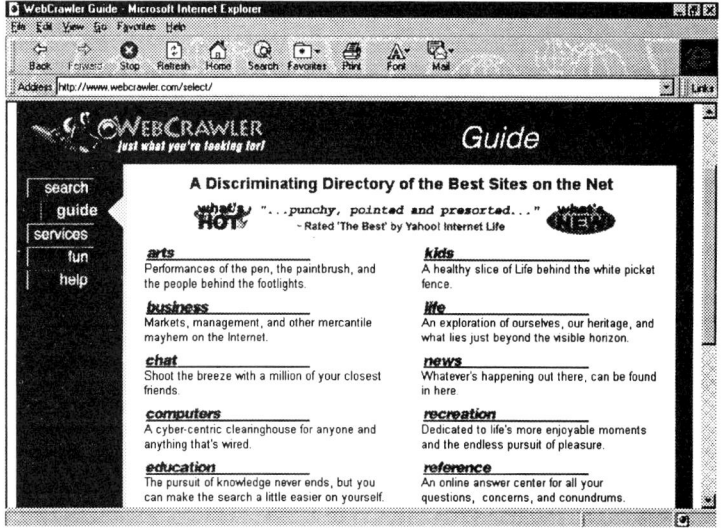

Selecting a Guide calls up a page containing a list of available subcategories. Each Guide area also features a weekly "best of" Web site which is displayed together with a brief review. The Guides are well organised and make looking for information on general topics quite easy.

WebCrawler services

In addition to search and directory features, Web Crawler offers a great deal of original material, including online classifieds, online news, weather and entertainment (including horoscopes). It also offers interactive maps and an online stock quote service, but these services are of limited use to non-US Internet users.

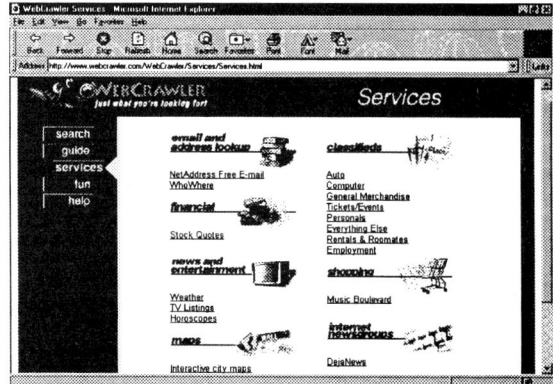

Chapter 11

Lycos

The name Lycos is derived from *Lycosidae*, a family of wolf spiders noted for actively pursuing prey, rather than relying on the more passive device of a web. This family of spiders, which is closely related to the Tarantula, is also well regarded for its speed over the ground. Presumably, Lycos' creators hoped that their choice of name would appeal to Internet users who want to actively locate information.

For many years, Lycos sported a spider-like logo, although it has recently abandoned this in favour of a less ferocious-looking icon.

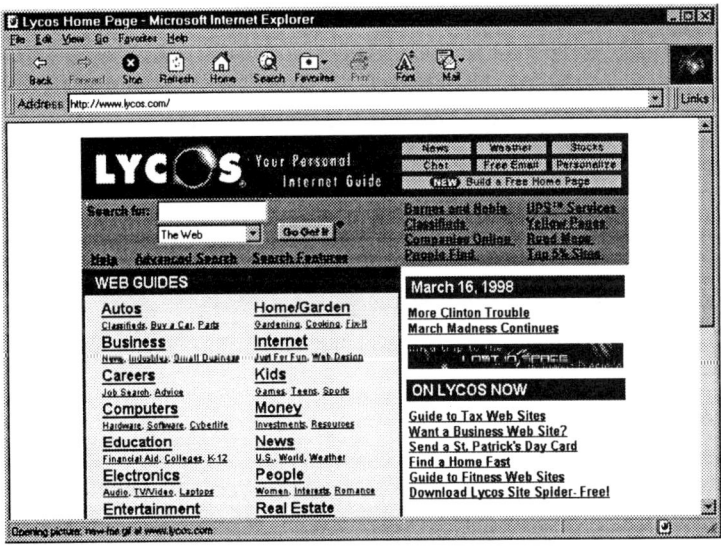

The Lycos Search Engine at http://www.lycos.com

Search with Lycos

Lycos caters for both keyword searches and browsing. The main Web page features a search box, 18 directory headings and links to free software, online classifieds and a Web-based Yellow Pages service.

Search basics

Lycos' extensive database contains the full text of every Web site and document it has indexed. However, redundant words, such as "the", "and" and "a" have been purged. Therefore, it will ignore these words if you use them as part of your search query.

Search terms are entered in the text box, and searches are initiated by clicking on the *Go Get It* icon.

Using the pull-down menu next to the text box, you can restrict Lycos to searching the Web (the default), or for picture and sound (multimedia) files only or the Lycos "Top 5%" (its review of the best of the Web).

Advanced search options

Lycos supports a number of search operators, including:

- **Full Stop** or **Period** ("**.**"): When a full stop is placed at the end of a word, Lycos will only search for exact matches of the word. For instance, if you want to find Web sites with information on *season* but not *seasons*, use *season.* as your search term.
- **Excluded words:** To exclude words from Lycos searches, use the – sign. For example, *season –salt*
- **Partial words:** To allow Lycos to match partial words, use the **$** symbol. For example, *pig$* would find *pig*, *piggery* and *pigeon*. This can be useful when you are searching for someone by name, but are not certain of the correct spelling.

Browsing Lycos' directory

Lycos features an easily navigable directory of sites, listed under categories such as *Technology, Education, Shopping* and *Science*.

Selecting *Education*, for example, displays the Lycos *Education Guide* (shown in the screenshot below), which features current education-related news from around the globe, links to other education-related Lycos content, and links to sites featured in the Lycos "Top 5%" education area.

Each directory heading is linked to a resources page that contains news of current events, links to the best sites, and details of other Lycos offerings.

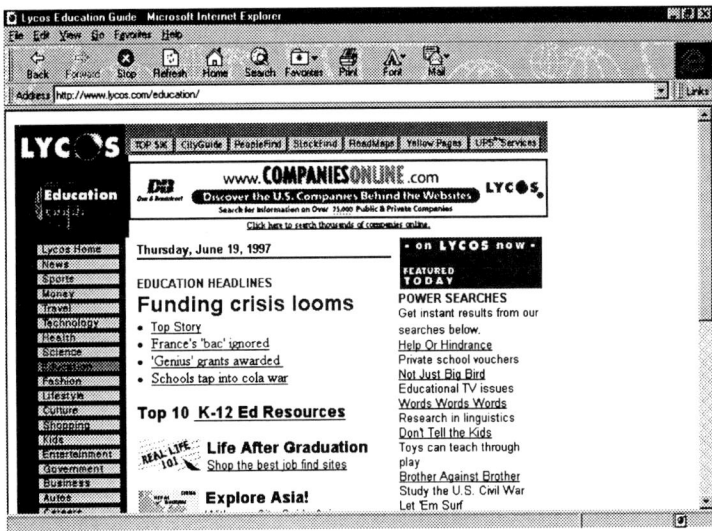

The Lycos Education Guide contains handy links to many education topics and sites

Lycos Custom Searches

Lycos offers a Custom Search page, currently available at:
http://lycospro.lycos.com/lycospro-nojava.html.

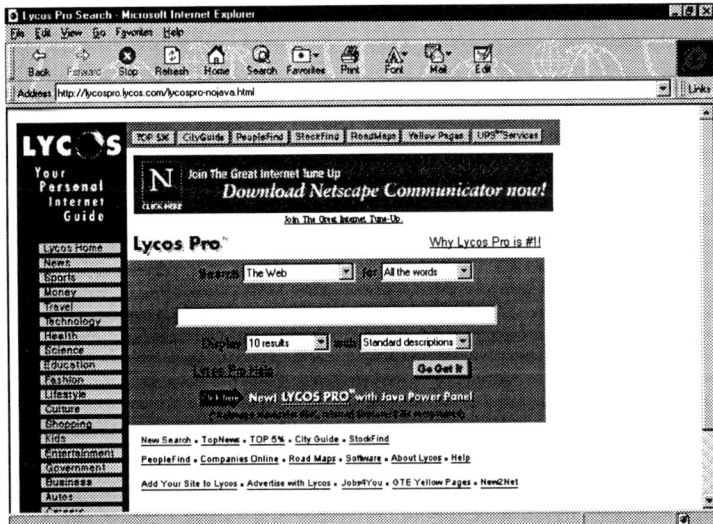

You can link to it from the main Lycos Web site by clicking on the Lycos Pro hyperlink immediately beneath the text box.

Using this page, you can modify the following options:

- **Search:** Choose to search the Web, Lycos' multimedia database for picture or sound files or Lycos' "Top 5%" directories. Lycos does not support Usenet searches at this stage.
- **Options:** Select whether Lycos should use an AND or an OR search as the default; that is whether it should search for *All the words* or *Any of the words*
- **Display:** Modify the number of hits that Lycos displays per page of results.
- **Results:** Choose between standard, summary and detailed results. This affects the amount of detail displayed about matched sites.

Lycos Pro Java Power Panel

If your Web browser supports Java (as the most recent versions of Netscape and Internet Explorer do), you can take advantage of the Lycos Pro with Java Power Panel.

You can connect to this site by typing in the URL:

http://lycospro.lycos.com/lycospro.html

or simply follow the link from the main Lycos Web site.

This search interface (shown on the following page) uses the familiar text-box and pull-down menus, but also features several "sliding rules". These can be used to vary the relative importance of certain search parameters. For instance, you can vary the frequency of matched words and determine how close your search terms should be found together on matched Web pages.

This is an excellent tool for users familiar with advanced search options, allowing greater control over the matching process than is currently available using operators.

Lycos 'Top 5%'

If you want quality matches (rather than quantity), look no further than Lycos' "Top 5%" directory. Lycos maintains a database of sites chosen by its staff of Web surfers for quality content, design and overall user-friendliness. Sites are rated out of 100, with a score of 100 designating "perfection".

Lycos

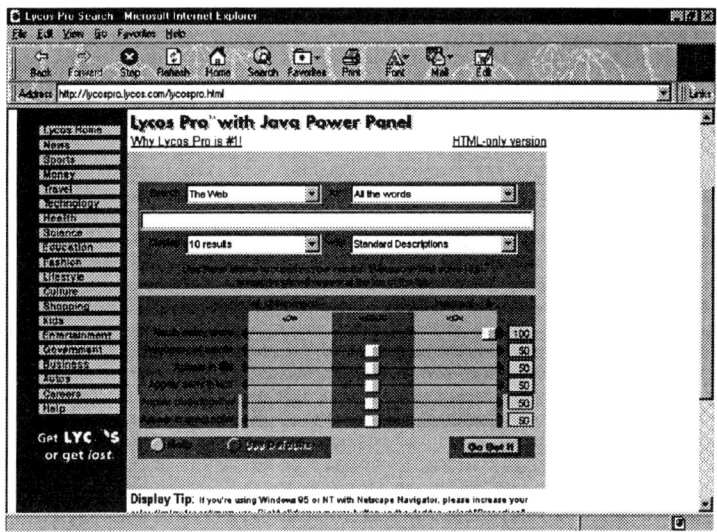

Lycos Pro's Java Power Panel lets you determine a number of search parameters

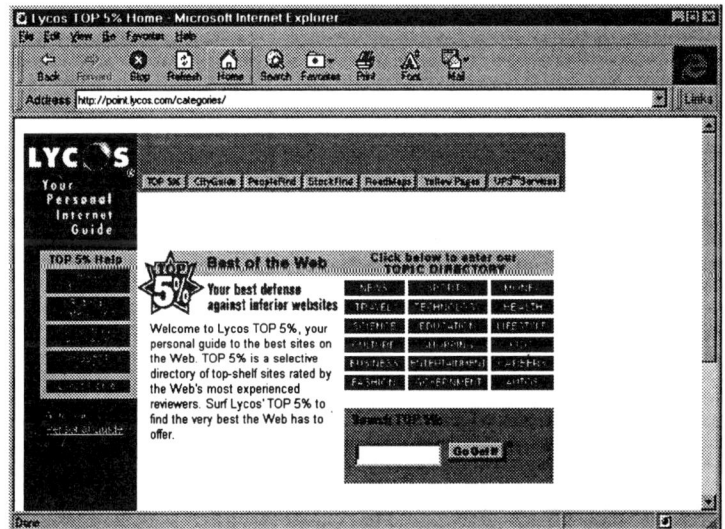

The Lycos 'Top 5%' directory is handy for locating quality sites

Chapter 12

InfoSeek

InfoSeek (at least in its current genesis) is perhaps best described as "utilitarian", as it lacks the glossy, graphic-laden look and feel of other major Search Engines. In fact, its directory layout and minimal use of graphics is reminiscent of Yahoo!, long recognised for its simplistic, non-crowded interface.

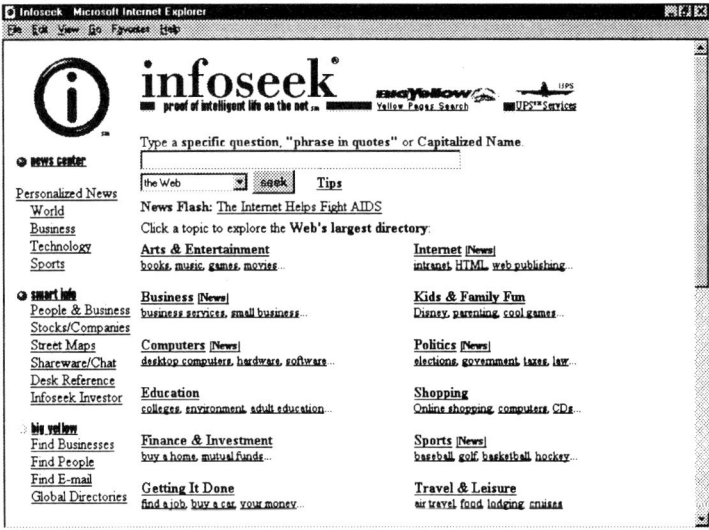

The InfoSeek Search Engine is located at http://www.infoseek.com

But don't let the façade fool you. InfoSeek is a very powerful and wide-ranging Search Engine. It was founded in January 1994 with one guiding principle: to provide Internet users with access to quality information that is also useful. InfoSeek certainly embraces this principle.

Seeking information with InfoSeek

InfoSeek's main Web site offers three "layers" of information. Firstly, there is the standard search box and directory listing. Then, you will find links to its "premium" information sites (basically guides to the best sites), as well as to online directories of business, people and email addresses.

InfoSeek also has a multicultural flavour, offering versions of the site in French, German, Italian and Japanese. You will also find a specific UK site (with a less US-centric outlook) at **www.infoseek.co.uk**.

Basic searches

The main page of InfoSeek offers a list of 13 directory headings for browsing, as well as a search box.

To initiate a basic search, type a query into the text box and click on the *Seek* button. To refine the scope of the search, click on the pull-down menu next to the *Seek* icon. You will be presented with a choice of areas in which to search:

- **The Web:** This is the default option, and prompts InfoSeek to search its extensive database of Web sites and their content.
- **Usenet Newsgroups:** Limits your search to the content of Usenet newsgroups.
- **News Wires:** Limits your search to a collection of "news wires" from original news sources, such as Reuters, Business and PR Newswire. This allows you to track news issues even though the particular "wires" have not been featured in mainstream publications.
- **Premier News:** Search the daily news from seven major news sources, including CNN, The New York Times and The Washington Post.
- **Industry News:** Search the daily stories from a number of major sources of trade and industry newswires - a great way to keep up with the happenings in your industry or sector.
- **Email Addresses:** Search for the email address of a friend or colleague.
- **Company Capsules:** Access online databases containing information on thousands of (primarily US) companies.
- **Web FAQs:** Search a collection of FAQs posted to Usenet for information relevant to your search query. FAQs (which stands for Frequently Asked Questions) are information files containing common questions regarding a specific topic and answers to these questions. There are hundreds of FAQs available online, covering a broad spectrum of topics.

Advanced search options

- **Default search criteria:** InfoSeek uses OR - that is, it will search for Web sites matching any one of your search terms.
- **Quotations:** To specify words that must appear together, position them in quotation marks or link them with hyphens: *"three blind mice"*, or *three-blind-mice*.
- **Capitalise:** If you capitalise adjacent words, InfoSeek will treat them as a name or a title. For example, InfoSeek would distinguish between *River Phoenix* and *river phoenix*, with the first query returning matches relating to the late actor, the other concerning landmarks in a US city.
- **Specific Inclusions:** To specify a word that must appear in all matched documents, place a + before it. For example, if you wanted to find information about London Tower, while avoiding any general geological references, you would use *london +tower*

Web-specific search options

InfoSeek supports a number of operators that restrict searches to specific portions of Web sites or documents:

- **link:**net-works.co.uk

Matches Web sites that contain at least one link to the specified domain name or Web site. Here the site specified is net-works.co.uk. This is useful for finding reviews of your favourite Web sites and resources.

- **site:**microsoft.com

Limits the search to information contained on a specific Web site.

- **URL:**net-works

Matches Web sites or pages which contain the specified word in their URL.

- **title:**net-works

Locates Web sites or pages with the specified word in their title.

Although InfoSeek has the text of 1.5 million sites indexed in full and 10 million more indexed using keywords, it is not the best tool for comprehensive searches, as even these impressive figures pale in comparison with the other major Search Engines. However, for speed, relevancy and currency, it's hard to beat.

InfoSeek directories

InfoSeek's directory structure is similar to that of other popular Search Engines.

Clicking on the directory heading will link you to a page containing a detailed list of sub-headings. From there you can jump to pages containing more specific headings and individual site listings.

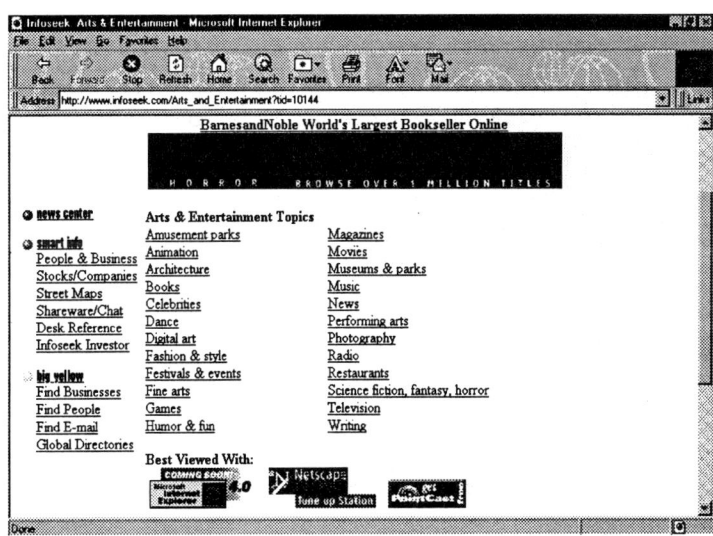

The InfoSeek Arts and Entertainment sub-directory contains a detailed list of sub-headings, from which you can jump to pages containing more specific headings and individual site listings

Additional InfoSeek services

In addition to search functions and directory listings, InfoSeek offers several online content areas.

These include up-to-the-minute news services (covering world, politics, business, sports and entertainment news), movie guides, weather information (US only), a searchable online dictionary and thesaurus, as well as links to streetmaps (US-centric), shareware, a Yellow Pages service (US-centric), discussion areas and share information.

Tip

For more information regarding how Search Engines work, visit The Spider's Apprentice: http://www.monash.com/spidap.html

Chapter 13

Meta-Search Engines

Meta-Search Engines are a Web-search enthusiasts' friend. Using Meta-Search Engines can cut valuable hours off your research time. How?

A Meta-Search Engine is not a true Search Engine. It does not have its own database of sites, nor does it employ a search spider. Instead, Meta-Search Engines exist to help users search multiple Search Engines at the same time.

In essence, a Meta-Search Engine submits your search query to a number of different Search Engines. It then collates and displays the results it receives.

Dogpile

Dogpile is the answer Aaron Flin came up with when, frustrated with using Search Engines, he proclaimed, "There *must* be a better way!"

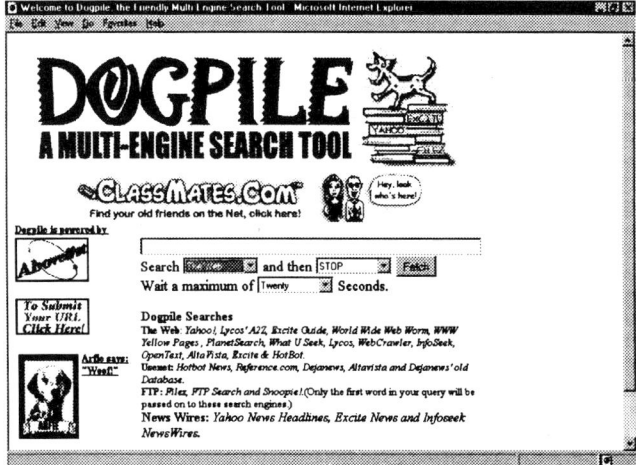

The unfortunately-named Meta-Search Engine at http://www.dogpile.com

Meta-Search Engines

Tired of searching one Search Engine only to find few or no matches, then receiving tens of thousands of matches from another, Flin decided to create a Meta-Search Engine to provide users with the best of every world.

From the main search screen of Dogpile you can specify your search query and modify several search options. These include deciding whether to search the Web, Usenet, ftp servers or Newswires for matches. Impressively, Dogpile allows you to search two different areas at once. You can also specify how long Dogpile should wait for a response from each Search Engine (between 10 and 60 seconds).

Once Dogpile has polled the various Search Engines (it accessed 25 major Search Engines at the time of writing), it displays the results, divided into sections according to the Search Engine that reported them.

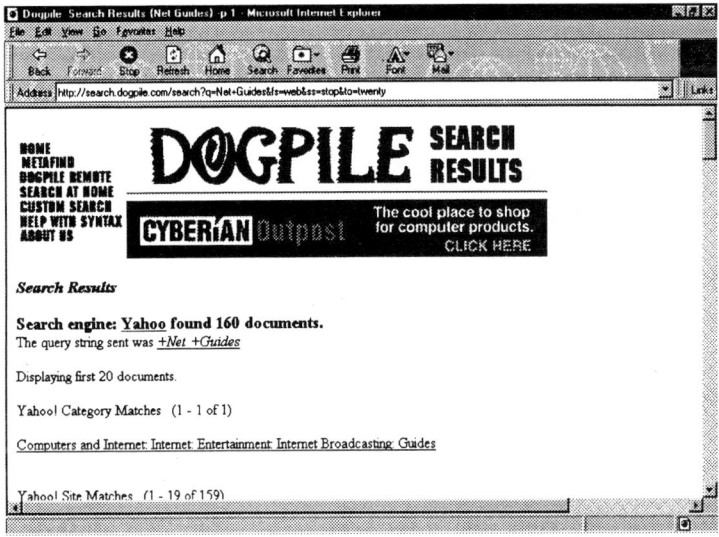

Dogpile does not actually search all 25 Search Engines at once. Instead, it submits your search query to the first three Engines on its list. If these do not record at least 10 hits, it moves on to the next three Search Engines.

Once it records at least 10 hits, Dogpile stops to display the details. It will continue polling the next set of Search Engines when you click on the *Next Set of Search Engines* button at the bottom on the search results page.

Metasearch.com

Metasearch offers a unique twist to "polling" various Search Engines. Instead of passing your search query on to a number of Search Engines, Metasearch analyses your query and then displays a page containing search boxes linked to several major Search Engines (such as Yahoo!, AltaVista, Lycos and WebCrawler).

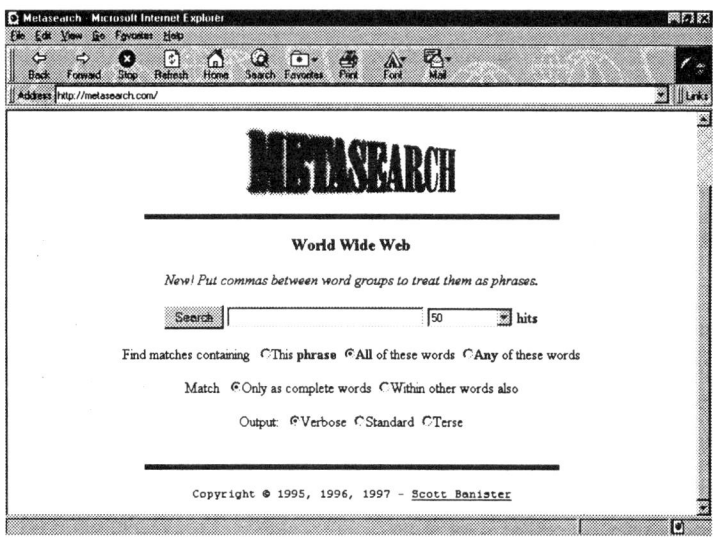

The Metasearch Search Engine at http://metasearch.com offers a unique twist to searching the Web

Each search box contains your query modified to reflect the most appropriate format for use with that Search Engine. Regardless of whether your query is entered in plain English or using operators, Metasearch devises the appropriate format for each Search Engine (usually both quickly and accurately).

To submit your newly streamlined search query, simply click on the *Search* button next to the logo of each Search Engine.

In the unlikely event that you want to further refine your query, you have access to a number of buttons or pull-down menus appropriate to each Search Engine.

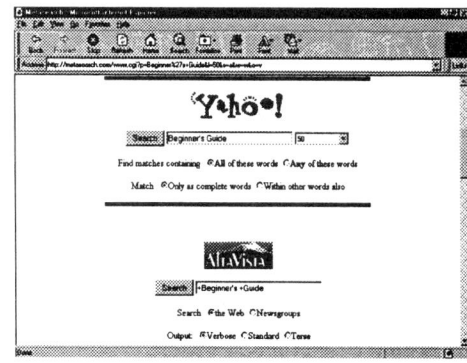

MetaCrawler

MetaCrawler was conceived as a Master's Degree project by Erik Selberg and his advisor, Oren Etzioni, at the University of Washington. At the time of writing, it encompassed six major Search Engines: Yahoo!, AltaVista, Excite, InfoSeek, WebCrawler and Lycos.

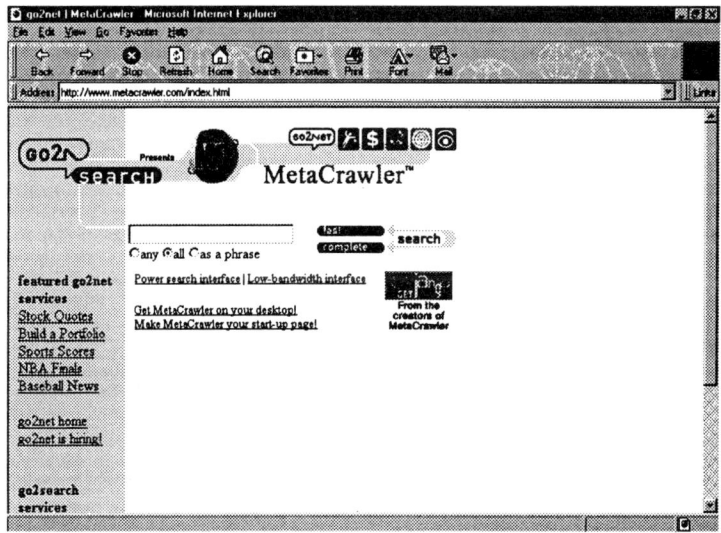

The MetaCrawler Meta-Search Engine at http://www.metacrawler.com

Composing searches is simple. Type your search term(s) in the text box provided, and toggle the "any", "all" or "as a phrase" search options. You also have the option of searching the Web, Usenet or for shareware programs. Once you are happy with your search query, click on *Search*.

MetaCrawler submits your query to the Search Engines in the most appropriate format. More importantly, it reorders all hits in terms of relevancy, removes duplicate matches, and displays the results as a single prioritised list. As such, MetaCrawler is an indispensable tool for Internet researchers.

Internet Sleuth

Internet Sleuth is something of a mixed bag. Although it claims to work with over 2,000 Search Engines may sound incredible, this is not in fact stretching the truth!

Find What You Want on the Internet

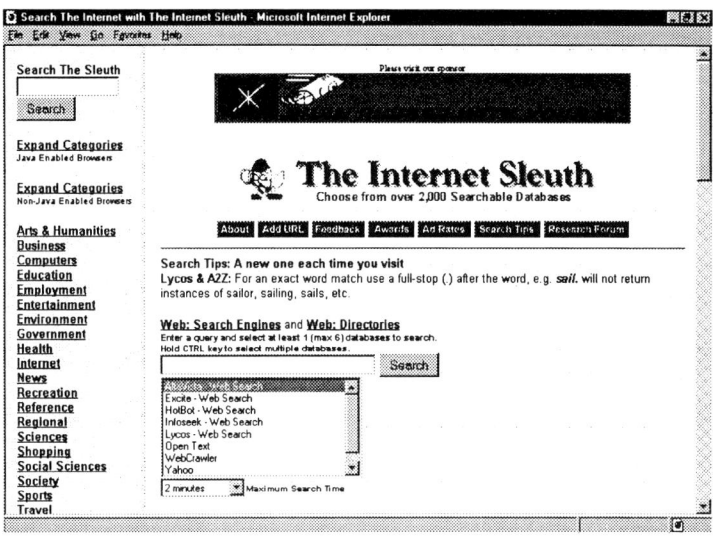

'Seek and ye shall find' at Internet Sleuth (http://www.isleuth.com)

Searching with Internet Sleuth

The main Web site provides users with six major search areas: *Web Engines and Directories*, *Web Review Sites*, *Online News Sources*, *Business and Finance Resources*, *Software Archives* and *Usenet News*. Within each search area, a number of different sites are available for searching.

Searching multiple sites is easy. Type your search term into the text box provided, and click on the resource you wish to search. To search multiple resources, hold down Ctrl as you select the resources (each chosen resource will be greyed out). Lastly, select how long you are prepared to wait for the search results (up to five minutes) and then click on the *Search* button.

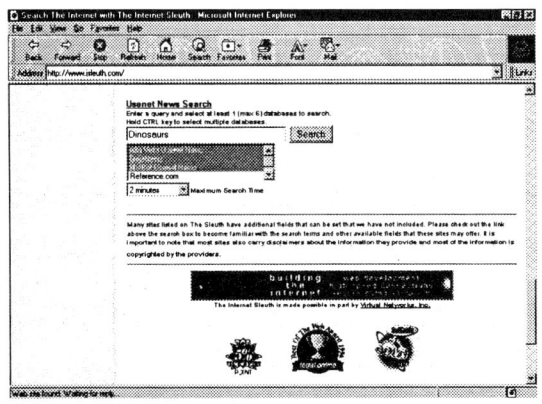

Searching multiple Usenet resources is easy with Internet Sleuth

Meta-Search Engines

Results from the first Search Engine or Web resource will be displayed on a single page. If more than one page of matches is retrieved, these will be accessible via links. If you have chosen to search more than one resource, results from these can be accessed by clicking the appropriate links.

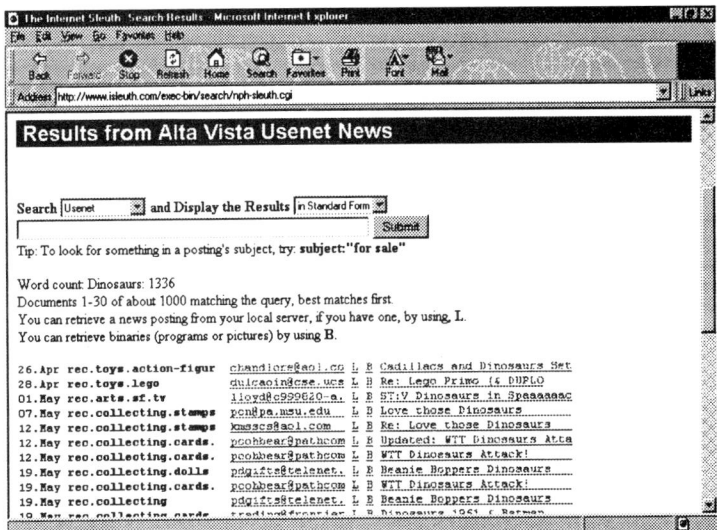

The results from the first Search Engine or Web resource will be displayed on a single page in Internet Sleuth. If more than one page of matches is retrieved, there will be links to additional pages

Browsing with Internet Sleuth

Internet Sleuth offers a comprehensive, browse-able list of subject categories, which you will see arranged along the left-hand side of the Web site. Clicking on a subject category will take you to a search page.

However, rather than offering the major Web Search Engines and resources, these subject search pages display menus of sites containing information related to the category.

For example, the *Arts and Humanities* category area (shown in the screenshot below) lists a collection of online arts databases and arts-specific Search Engines on a single page, thereby providing links to other major sources of information relevant to your interests.

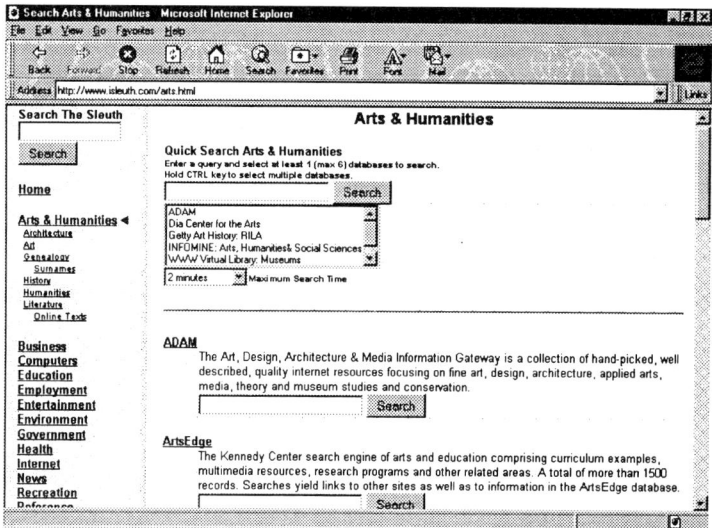

You'll find links galore listed under each Internet Sleuth category

Inference Find

Inference Find works with the six largest Search Engines - WebCrawler, Yahoo!, Lycos, AltaVista, InfoSeek, and Excite. Each of these Search Engines is polled by Inference Find at the same time, thereby reducing search delays.

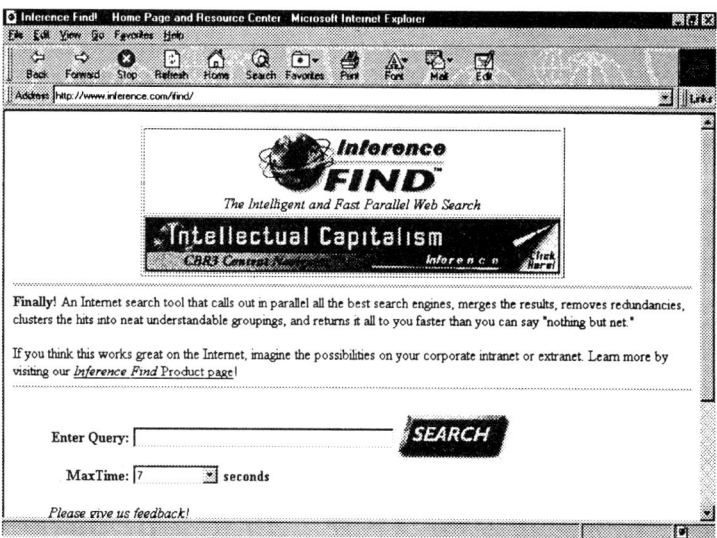

The Inference Find Meta-Search Engine at http://www.inference.com/ifind/

To enhance the search process, Inference Find merges the results reported by the different Search Engines, removes duplicate matches, and displays the results according to relevance. (Relevance, it should be added, is determined by Inference Find.)

In order to maximise the potential of each query, Inference Find will poll some Search Engines several times.

For instance, whereas Yahoo! allows you to request 100 matches per page, InfoSeek will only display 10 results at a time. So Inference Find will query InfoSeek several times, in order to extract a larger number of matches.

> *TIP*
>
> Meta-Search Engines can be a godsend when time is limited. But they do have an Achilles' heel that it pays to keep in mind. Search Engines vary subtly in their responses to search terms, and their use of operators. If a Meta-Search Engine is not correctly programmed to use the appropriate search modifiers, it may return negative or inaccurate search results for a particular Search Engine.

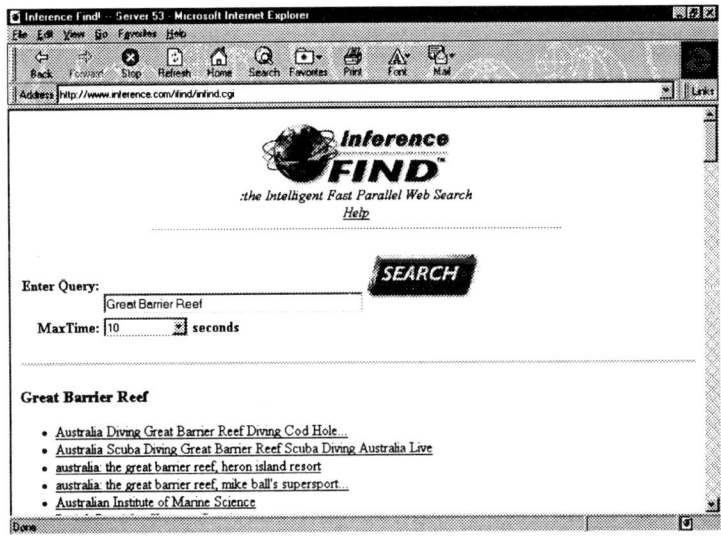

Inference Find's results page makes navigating matched sites easy

ProFusion

ProFusion is certainly not the prettiest search interface, but what it lacks in design and layout it makes up for in raw power.

Find What You Want on the Internet

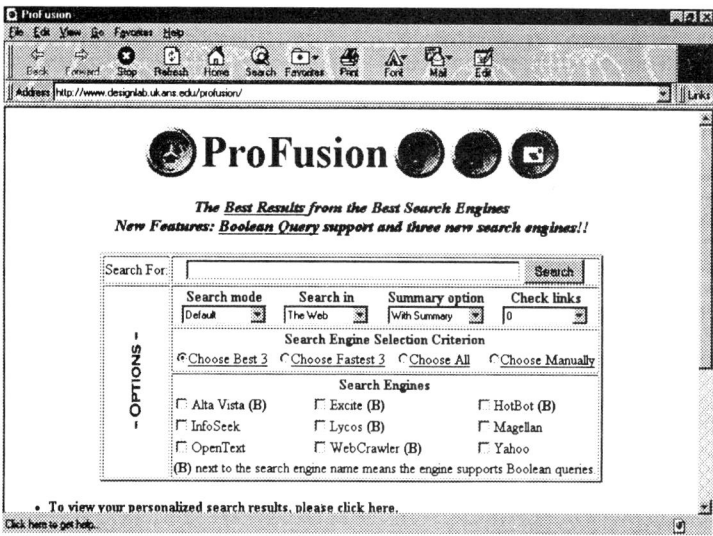

Not the prettiest site, but still powerful
(http://www.designlab.ukans.edu/profusion/)

ProFusion supports several Search Engines, including Excite, InfoSeek, Lycos, WebCrawler and AltaVista. It operates in much the same fashion as other Meta-Search Engines, combining results and removing duplicate matches. Profusion supports both Web and Usenet searches.

However, ProFusion offers two important services, discussed below.

Automatic Pick Best 3

ProFusion analyses your search query, then selects which of the Search Engines that it supports will give the best results. It will use these for your search.

Users can disable this service, in which case ProFusion will use all supported Search Engines.

Personalised searches

ProFusion allows users to register with its free personalised search service, which records details of frequent searches. Users can later return to the site and ask it to automatically perform these registered searches. This is a useful and time-effective way to monitor Web sites to see whether they have new or updated information on your research topic.

TIP

Want to really save time? Why not install your very own Meta-Search Engine, and use it to search up to eight Search Engines at a time? Download Search4 from http://www.intermania.com/

Chapter 14

Intelligent Search Agents

There can be no doubt that Search Engines have made locating information and Web sites easier than ever before. In the space of a few seconds, Internet users can now search through tens of millions of pages of information—a task that would take several lifetimes if performed manually.

It doesn't get any better than this. Or does it?

Necessity is the mother of invention

Search Engines, for all their power and speed, are inflexible. Users need to spend time learning the particular nuances of each Search Engine, coming to grips with any special search requirements it may have, and understanding its strengths and weaknesses.

Because of the effort required to truly master and efficiently use a Search Engine, most Internet users rarely enlist the support of more than one or two. As a result, it's a real possibility that important Internet resources will remain undiscovered.

Meta-Search Search Engines go some way towards breaching the gap between skilled and novice Internet users, but their interaction with Search Engines is often clumsy, especially when they have not been updated to reflect new search options and procedures supported by the Search Engines they use.

Information-hungry users demand a better way.

Intelligent Agent technology, it seems, is the ideal solution.

Intelligent Agents can be best thought of as the digital equivalent of exceptionally intelligent and faithful golden retrievers. They are software programs designed to "learn" as much as possible about your interests, your style of expressing yourself, and your information requirements.

A typical Intelligent Agent scenario unfolds as follows:

Once installed, the Intelligent Agent program begins to develop a profile of your interests, either by posing a series of questions, or displaying a list of topics for you to rank in order of importance.

The Intelligent Agent then sits back and watches, over your shoulder as it were, as you go about your normal Internet travels. It pays particular attention to the types of Web sites you visit, the Usenet newsgroups you read and the sorts of information you access.

Having analysed your information requirements and online habits, the Intelligent Agent is ready to roam the Internet in search of useful titbits of information and other resources. Every now and then it will send you an email message summarising its latest findings, listing the sites it has visited, the information they contain and why it thinks you will find them useful.

The future today

Sound too sci-fi to believe? Well, you're right - at least in part.

Intelligent Agents have been with us for several years now, and have only recently begun to approach the level of sophistication described above. Although current versions do demonstrate certain levels of "artificial intelligence" and autonomy, we are still several years away from personalised, independent information agents.

However, some of the Intelligent Agents available now are still a useful addition to your information-searching system. They will, for example, scour Search Engines and other online directories, looking for sites relevant to your search queries, although they still rely greatly on your involvement, both in deciding where to look and what to look for. But, correctly implemented, these programs are not only fun to use, but also offer powerful search functions.

Agentware

Site: http://www.agentware.com
Program: Agentware Desktop Suite v.1.5
Operating System: Windows 3.11 or Windows 95
File Size: 4.5Mb (compressed)

Intelligent Search Agents

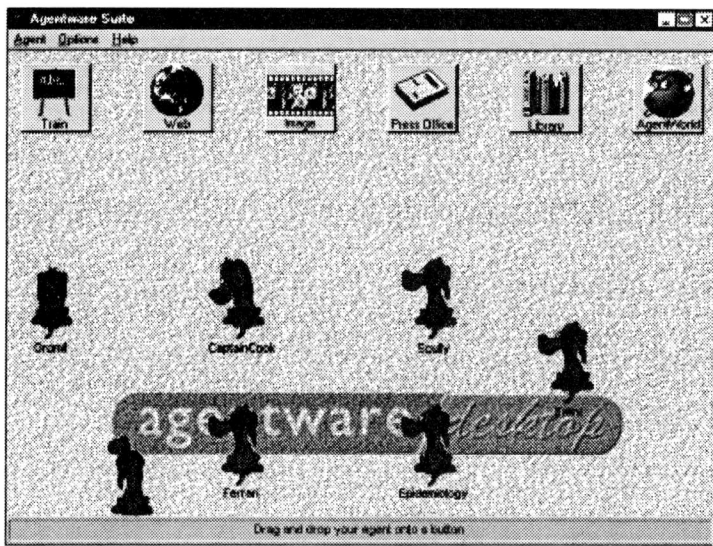

Agentware's point-and-click interface makes it easy to use

Agentware (desktop edition) is an excellent example of how Intelligent Agents can make life much easier for both the novice and advanced Internet user.

Having downloaded and installed Agentware, your first job is to *train* a new agent for use.

To do this, select *Agent* then *New* from the menu bar. The *New Agent* window (shown below) will appear, prompting you to specify a name for your new agent. You can call it whatever you like - Rex, Fido or even Englebert - but it's generally a good idea to give it a name relevant to the searching it will be trained to do. I called my new agent *SpaceShuttle*, as I want to use it to find information relating to NASA's Space Shuttle project.

When using an Intelligent Agent be sure to give it a meaningful name!

The next step is to enter a "plain English" sentence describing the information you are looking for. I used: *I am looking for information relating to NASA's Space Shuttle project.*

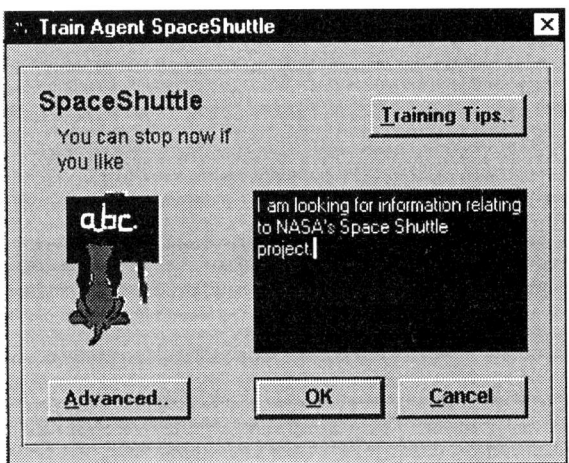

Now, click on the *OK* button. Your Agent will analyse your search request - and then the hunt is on!

Your Agent will appear on the main Agentware screen. To begin searching, select its icon and drag this onto the revolving globe icon.

The *Web Research* window will appear, keeping you informed of your Agent's progress. The name (and usually the URL) of each site that it contacts will be displayed, and matching sites will be displayed onscreen both in a list and graphically. A flashing green *Agent Alert* message will also appear to inform you that successful matches have been found.

To view the matched sites, click on the *Preview* button. A description of the site and its content will appear within the *Web Research* window. If a site looks like it will be of use to you, click on the *Add to Library* icon to save its details in Agentware's library.

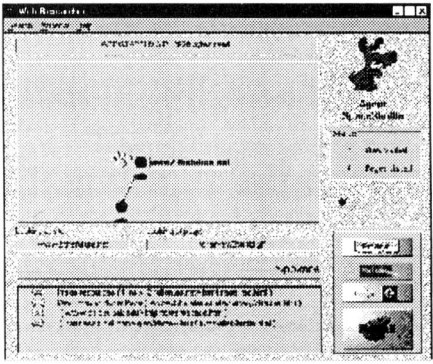

Your Agent will continue searching the Web until you recall it, which you do (appropriately) by clicking on the *Whistle* icon. However, you have to remain connected to the Internet while you have your Agent deployed.

CyberSearch

Site: http://www.frontiertech.com
Program: CyberSearch
Operating System: Windows 95 and Windows NT
File Size: 21Mb (compressed)

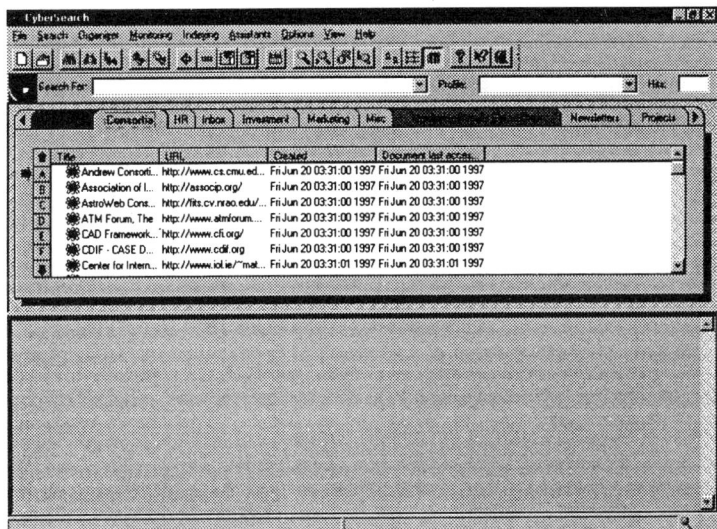

As you can see, CyberSearch is more than just a simple Agent program

CyberSearch is a huge program - at 21Mb, it takes around two hours to download over a fast modem connection - but, in my opinion, the program is worth every minute of the download time.

CyberSearch is more than just an Agent program. It is also a Web browser, a bookmark organiser, a personal Search Engine and a detailed database of valuable information sites. Briefly stated, CyberSearch is a one-stop shop for all your information and search needs.

To create your first Search Assistant using CyberSearch, click on *Assistants*, then select *Search Assistants Wizard*. The Search Assistant dialogue box will appear, prompting you to specify a name for your Search Assistant. Again, try to choose a name that will remind you of the type of information for which your Search Assistant is looking.

For this example, I will search for information on dinosaurs, so I will call my Search Assistant *Dinosaurs*. Once you have named your Search Assistant, click on the *Next* button.

Find What You Want on the Internet

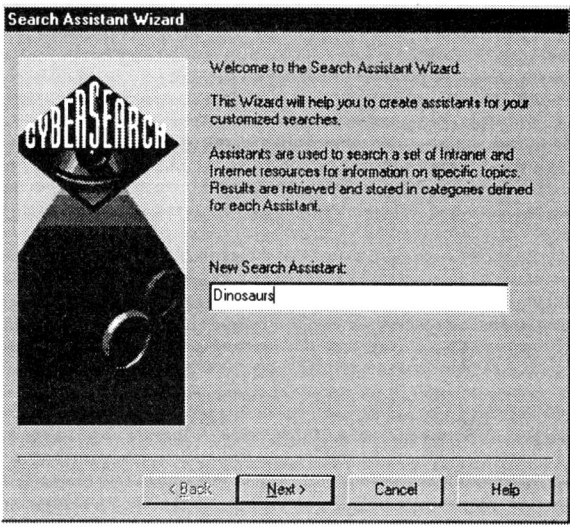

You are now prompted to specify your search term(s), and indicate whether you wish to limit the number of hits to be displayed. Once you have finished entering these details, click on the *Next* button.

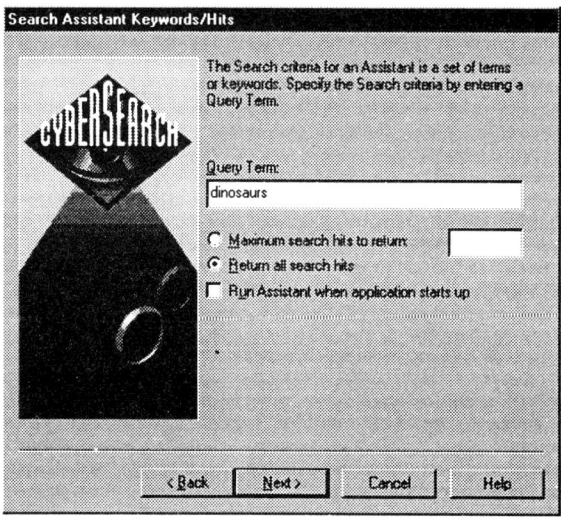

During the next stage, you will be prompted to select from the various search profiles available. By default, CyberSearch uses search profiles of six major Search Engines, including Yahoo!, AltaVista and Excite.

Tip
CyberSearch can be used to search for files and information on the Internet and on your own PC (or computer network).

You can create your own profiles, or include details of different Search Engines in a single profile. This allows you to search several Search Engines at the same time (as you would using a Meta-Search).

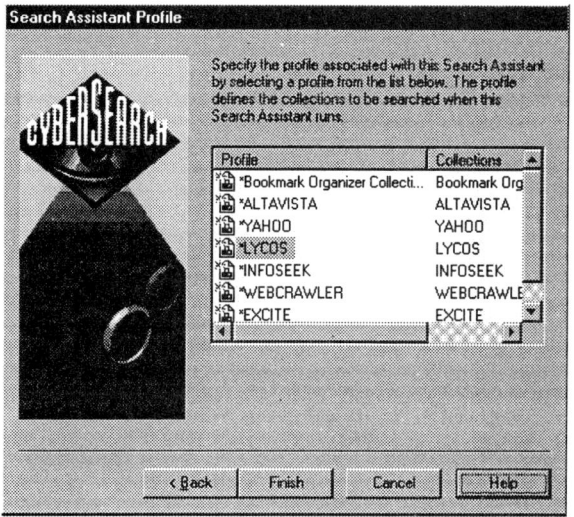

This screen is used to specify which Search Engines you want CyberSearch to search

Once you have selected your profile, click on *Finish*. Your Search Assistant is now ready for activation (you can check its details by clicking on the *Assistants* tab). To activate your Search Assistant, select *Search* from the menu bar, and then click on *Start Search Assistants*.

Within a minute or so, your Search Assistant will complete its search (although the time taken depends on the number of Search Engines in your search profile). The results are displayed under a new tab, which is given the same name as your Search Assistant.

Viewing a matched Web site is as simple as double-clicking on it in the list. Your Web browser will be launched, and the relevant Web page displayed.

Go-Get-It

Site: http://www.hpp.com
Program: Go-Get-It
Operating System: Windows 3.11, Windows 95 and Windows NT
File Size: 0.8Mb (compressed)

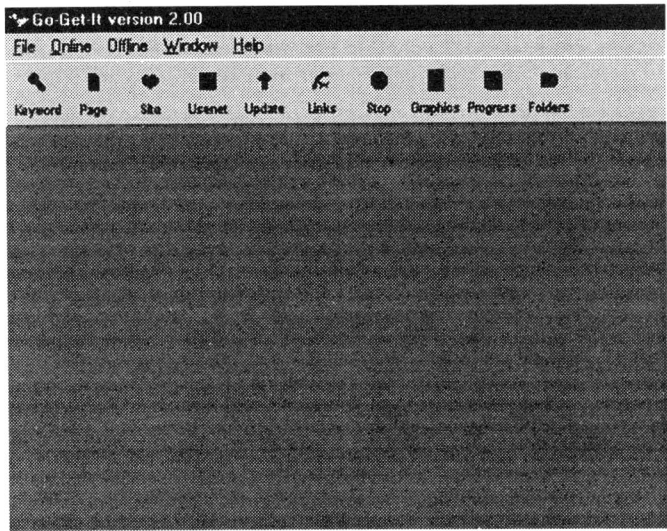

The Go-Get-It interface may be dowdy - but its search capabilities are powerful

Go-Get-It is a regular little dynamo. It allows you to search four major Search Engines in one go, scan Usenet newsgroups - even download entire Web sites for offline viewing! On top of all that, it allows you to run 10 different search queries at the same time. Talk about a time saver!

Go-Get-It's tool bar presents users with search options, including:

- **Keyword:** Used for keyword searches of multiple Search Engines.
- **Page:** To find only one or a few related Web sites or pages.
- **Site:** Enables you to download entire Web sites.
- **Usenet:** For Usenet keyword searches.
- **Progress:** Display a graphical representation of your search's progress.

To perform a keyword search of several Search Engines, click on the *Keyword* icon on the tool bar. Enter your search term(s) in the box provided and then click on *OK*. Click on *OK* again to begin the search.

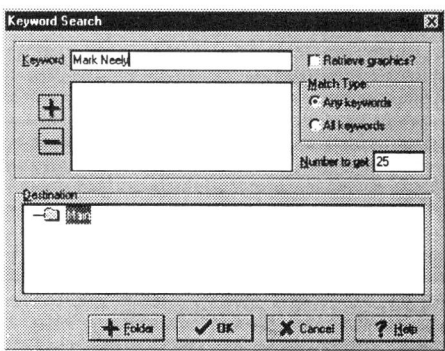

Intelligent Search Agents

Go-Get-It will connect to the first Search Engine on its list and perform a search. It will download the entire contents of any matched pages (including any associated graphics if you toggle the *Retrieve graphics* option). By default, Go-Get-It will only retrieve up to 25 matched documents, even if it finds more. You can change the maximum via the *Preferences* window.

Once Go-Get-It has finished searching, it stores all retrieved documents in the main folder, unless you specify a new folder name in the *Keyword* dialogue window. To view the contents, click on the *Folder* icon on the toolbar. To view a specific document, double-click on it.

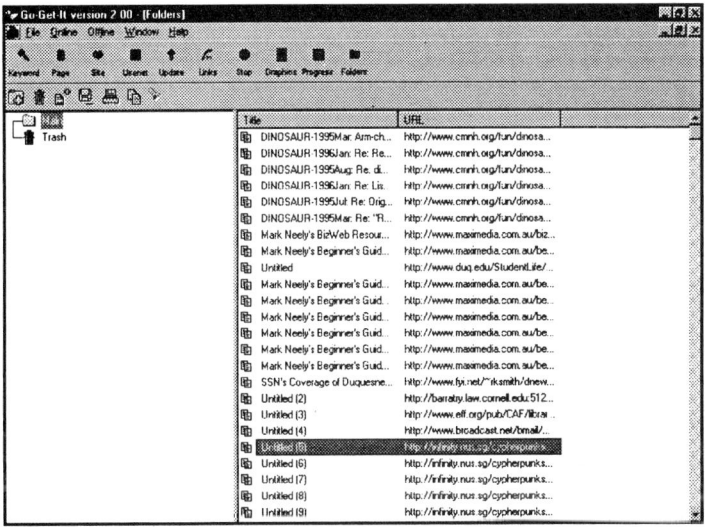

Chapter 15

Finding Someone Online

One of the most perplexing aspects of the Internet is that there is no easy way to ascertain someone's email address. There is no online equivalent of the phone book, where everyone's email address is listed.

There are a number of reasons for this, the main one being that there is no central authority charged with issuing email addresses (as there is - or was until recently - a sole source for telephone numbers). As such, no one is in a position to collate email addresses.

The best advice I can give to people who want to obtain someone's email address is to simply call that person and ask! Hardly the pinnacle of technological progress, but that's the way it is.

Email directories

Having said that, there are a number of email directories online that attempt to provide a White Pages solution for email addresses.

Basically, they are huge databases of email addresses collected over the years (we discuss how shortly). They have a simple search interface, in which you type the name of the individual whose address you are looking for. In this regard, the directories work quite well.

But they have a fundamental flaw.

There is no obligation for anyone to actually register with these directories. And, given that no one organisation officially collates email addresses, these directories have to find other means of collecting them.

Finding Someone Online

The standard trick is to filter Usenet postings, which usually contain both the name and email address of the person who posts a message. The problem with this is that not everyone uses Usenet, which means that there are many people whose email address you *won't* find using such services.

> **TIP**
>
> Although many people regard online 'people finder' databases as a convenient, free service, others find them intrusive—and who can blame them? It is now possible for US Internet users to search White Pages listings, and retrieve not only an individual's telephone number and street address, but also view a street map with the person's house marked with a cross!

But, if you are in a pinch and you need to find someone's email address (and cannot otherwise contact them), then email directories and email Search Engines are worth a shot.

BigFoot

BigFoot has been around for some time, and over the years has amassed quite a collection of email addresses.

BigFoot has one of the largest email address collections which you can find at http://www.bigfoot.com

In addition to providing email address search facilities, BigFoot allows users to search the White Pages (US-based), request email reminders of important dates and even apply for a free email address.

To search BigFoot's database, type the name in the text box, toggle the *Email* option, and click on the *Search* icon. BigFoot will then display a list of matches.

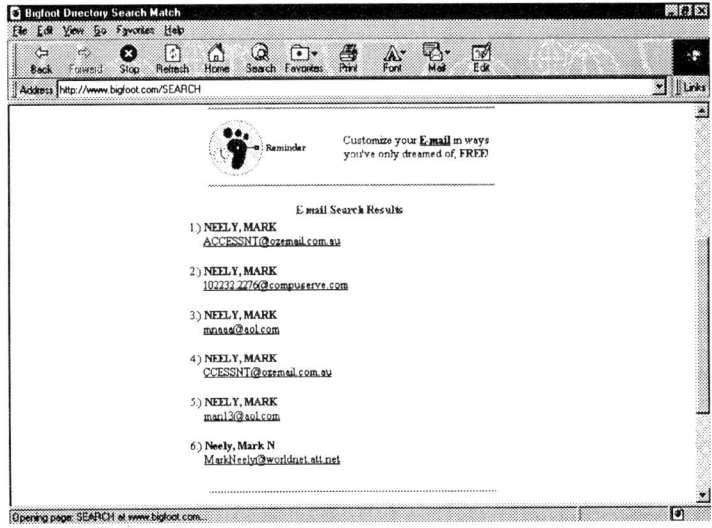

The only problem now is working out which is the right *Mark Neely!*

Meta Email Search Agent (MESA)

MESA is, in essence, a people-finding Meta-Search Engine.

MESA will submit your query to a number of different email directories and databases, and collate the results.

Remember, however, that by polling several databases at once, you not only increase the chance of finding a match, but also increase the chance that the matches you find *won't* be for the person you want to find. Determining which address is the right one is a matter of educated guesswork and following up leads.

TIP

It seems that, in a bid to become the biggest and the best, email directories have neglected their housekeeping. In researching this chapter, I came across a number of my former email accounts - some of which I have not used since my university days almost a decade ago!

Finding Someone Online

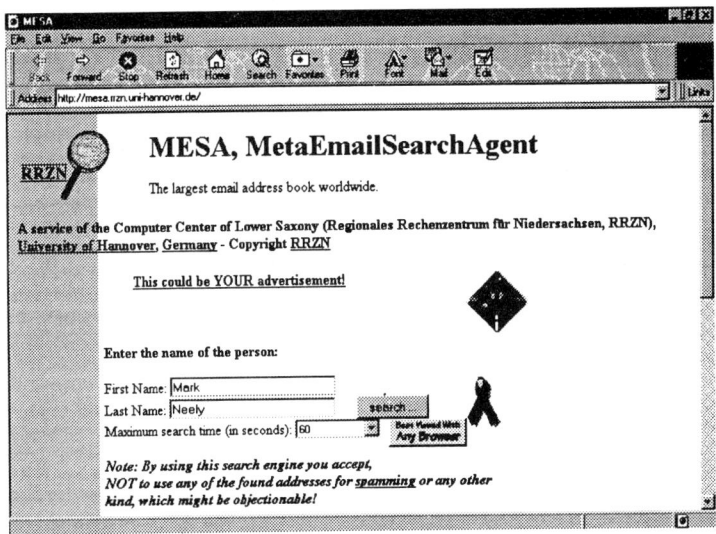

Use MESA to search several email directories at once. Find it at
http://mesa.rrzn.uni-hannover.de/

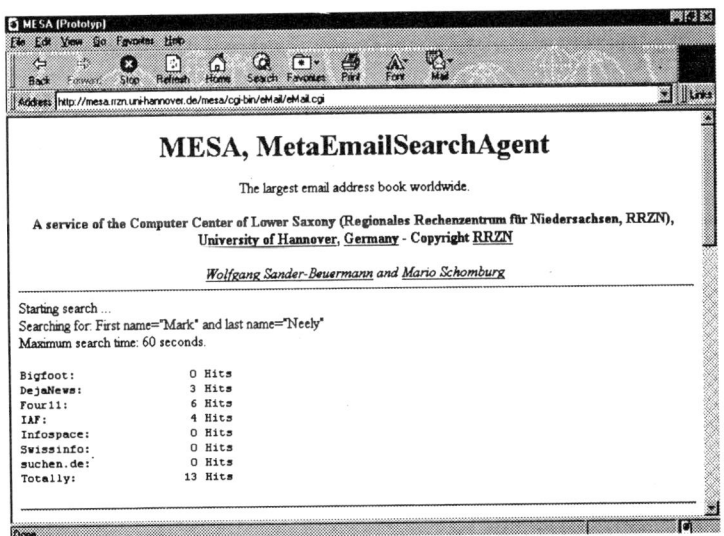

MESA found my email address, plus some very old, dormant addresses!

Four11

Four11 is one of the more sophisticated email directory services available online.

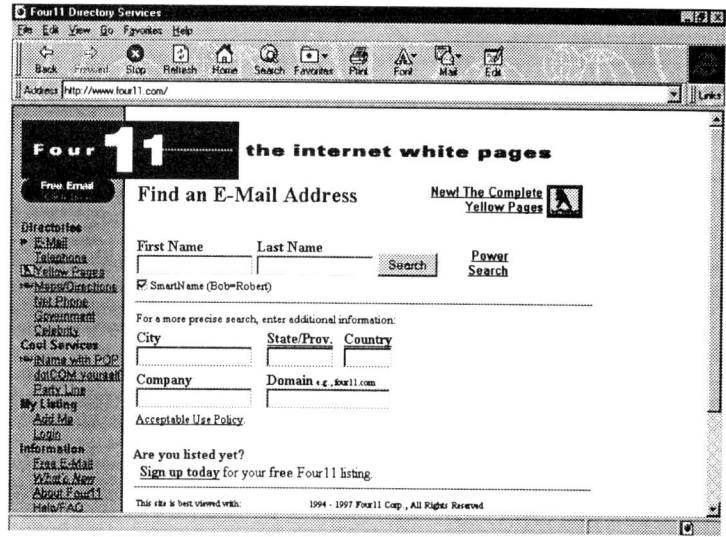

At http://www.four11.com/ you'll find Four11, one of the more sophisticated email Search Engines

Among the features it offers is the ability to limit searches by geographic region, domain name or company name. For instance, if you know Uncle Bob has an email account with *example.com.au*, or uses a company email account provided by Smith & Co., you can limit your search accordingly, thereby increasing the accuracy of results.

Four11 also uses "smart" name matching, with the result that, for example, searches for "Robert Smith" will also match "Bob Smith".

Yahoo! People Finder

Yahoo!, like Four11, can limit searches to specific domain names, and uses smart name matching.

Unfortunately, it suffers the same problem as other email address search services, in that it is unable to provide much information about the addresses it matches.

Finding Someone Online

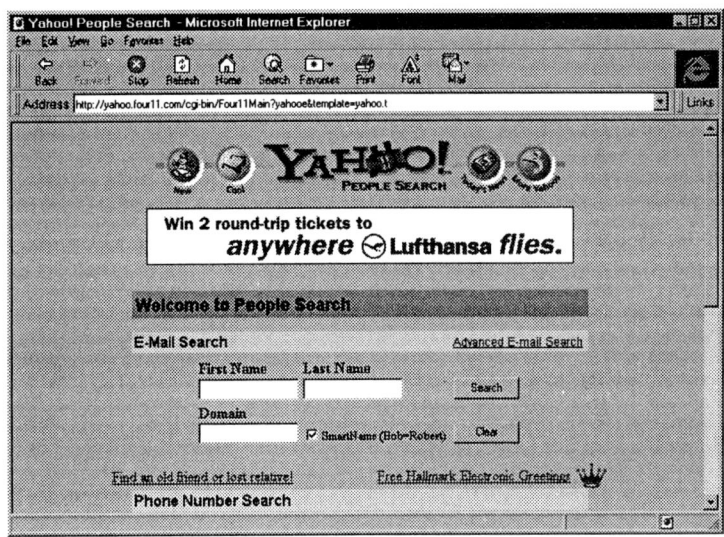

Yahoo! also provides an email search facility at http://www.yahoo.com/search/people/

Clicking on the person's name (which is displayed as a hyperlink) will take you to a second page, on which Yahoo! displays all that it knows about that person, including the country s/he lives in (and sometimes even a specific State or region).

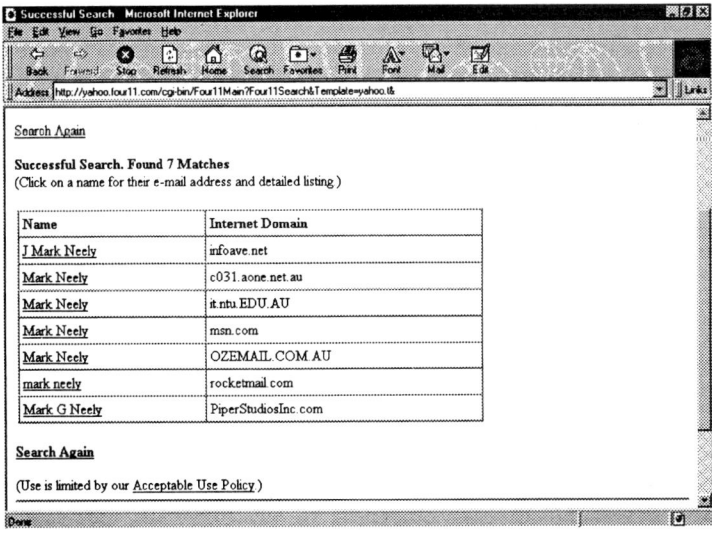

These results offer little assistance for guessing which address is the right one!

Chapter 16

Other Research Options

If you read through a collection of Internet magazines and books, you will be hard pressed to find information on Internet resources beyond the World Wide Web. The Web, it would seem, is the be-all-and-end-all of Internet resources. This attitude is not surprising - who can ignore the exciting, multimedia world of graphics, sound, images and text it offers?

However, by restricting your research to the Web alone, you may miss out on other important and potentially time-saving information resources.

This Chapter looks at three further avenues for information gathering: FAQs, email discussion groups and Usenet. It also takes a brief look at the world of online libraries.

Just the FAQs

The term FAQ stands for Frequently Asked Questions. A FAQ file, then, is a document that contains a list of frequently asked questions, and their answers. There are hundreds of FAQ files available on the Internet, covering a broad selection of topics.

FAQ files were created firstly to help fellow Internet users, and secondly to minimise time wasted answering questions posed by "newbies" (that is, inexperienced Internet users).

There are tens of thousands of newsgroups and email discussion groups available on the Internet, some of which discuss very specialised topics. Many of the regular participants have been following these discussion forums since their inception. Over the years, they have discussed dozens of topics, joined in heated debates, chastised members for inaccurate comments, and even taken time off for personal chit-chat and gossip.

Other Research Options

It soon became obvious to these "veterans" that each new generation of forum participants came in search of the same answers, and the forum was wasting time by answering the same questions time and again.

To solve this problem, participants volunteered to collectively author FAQ files, which all newcomers are invited (or occasionally *instructed*) to read before posting questions to the group. Newcomers usually find that their questions have been answered in the FAQ file and, having been brought up to speed, are able to join in the current discussions.

FAQ files therefore represent an excellent source of information.

Copies of FAQ files written for new participants in Usenet newsgroups are posted to the newsgroups on a regular basis (usually monthly, but occasionally weekly). You can also find a collection of FAQ files in the *news.answers* newsgroup, which is used as a central point of distribution for many FAQs.

> **TIP**
>
> Ask for help! It is unlikely that your problem is unique. Someone, somewhere, has probably succeeded after hours of trial and error in finding the information you seek. If your initial attempts turn up nothing, or are less satisfying than you had hoped, post a request for help in relevant newsgroups and email discussion lists.

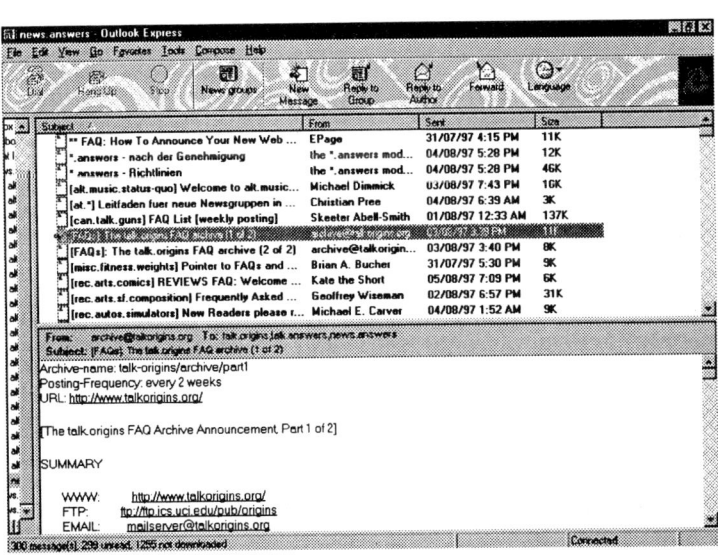

The news.answers Usenet newsgroup is an excellent source of FAQs

Find What You Want on the Internet

TIP

They just keep getting smarter! FAQFinder is an automated question-answerer. Users simply type in a question in plain English, and FAQFinder scours its database of FAQ files for the answer! Try it for yourself at http://infolab.cs.uchicago.edu/faqfinder/

Even though FAQ files are posted to Usenet newsgroups regularly, there is no guarantee that they will be available on the day you look for them. If they are not, you can search through one of the many FAQ archives available on the Web:

University of Michigan FAQ Archive:
http://faq.sph.umich.edu/cgi-bin/faqsrch
FAQ Finder:
http://ps.superb.net/FAQ/

The FAQ Finder Web site is both searchable and browse-able.

Other Research Options

Searchable list of Usenet FAQs:
http://www.cis.ohio-state.edu/hypertext/faq/usenet/top.html

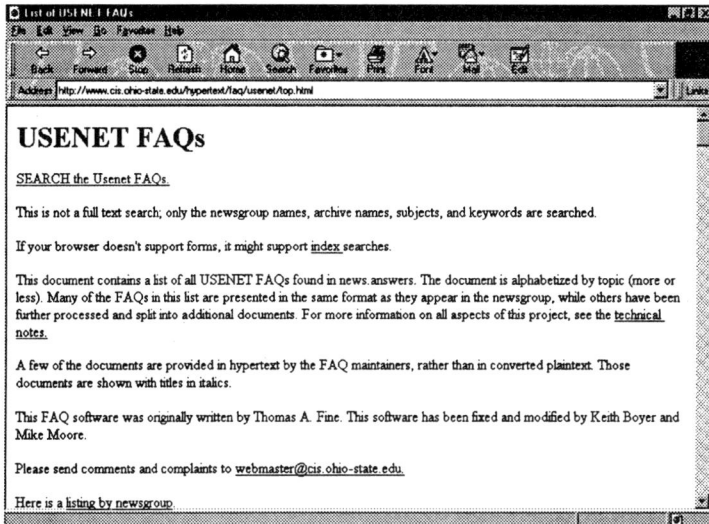

Oxford University's Search FAQ:
http://www.lib.ox.ac.uk/search/search_faqs.html

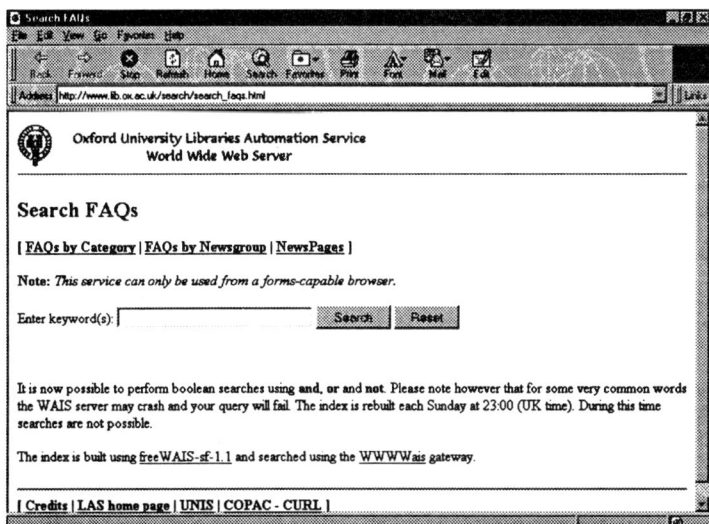

Most of these FAQ archives use basic "text string" matching search techniques. That is, they search each available FAQ to see if it contains any of the keywords you have specified. If it does, it is considered a match.

To avoid multiple irrelevant matches, avoid common terms (such as *and*, *FAQ*, *Usenet* and so on) and don't even bother with terms that are guaranteed to appear in every FAQ (such as *Internet*).

Email discussion groups

Email discussion groups are an excellent resource, both for a quick answer to a particular question and longer-term understanding or discussion of a topic in which you are interested.

Most email discussion groups are composed of two-way lists. That is, a copy of each message you send to the discussion group is sent to every other subscriber (and there may be thousands), and a copy of every message sent by every other subscriber is sent to you.

Some email discussion groups have a fairly low "traffic" rate; that is, they do not generate more than a handful of messages each week. Others, however, can generate 10, 20, even 50 messages each day.

Special email automation software is used to co-ordinate the discussion group. This software is in charge of adding new members to the group, and removing those who ask to leave.

Joining such groups usually involves sending an email message to a special email address, such as:

listserv@example.com.au

with a command in the body of your email similar to:

subscribe <name of list> Your Name

Newly formed email discussion groups are usually advertised (or "announced") via short postings to related Usenet newsgroups, outlining how interested users can subscribe or who to contact for further information. However, it is unusual for existing groups to be advertised (unless they are actively recruiting new members).

> *TIP*
>
> Even if you cannot find the answer to your question in a FAQ file, it will probably contain links to Web sites with related information. These pointers can help you to track down other useful resources.

Other Research Options

If you are successful in subscribing to (that is, joining) the discussion group, you will receive an email message from the discussion group automation software confirming your subscription. Read this message closely (and print a copy for safekeeping). It will contain administrative information, such as who to email in the event of problems, how to unsubscribe, and some general rules of behaviour. More importantly, you will usually be pointed to the discussion group's FAQ. Be sure to download and read this before posting any questions in the forum.

To find out more about how email discussion groups work, check out:

The International Federation of Library Associations and Institutions Internet Mailing Lists Guides and Resources

http://www.nlc-bnc.ca/ifla/I/training/listserv/lists.htm

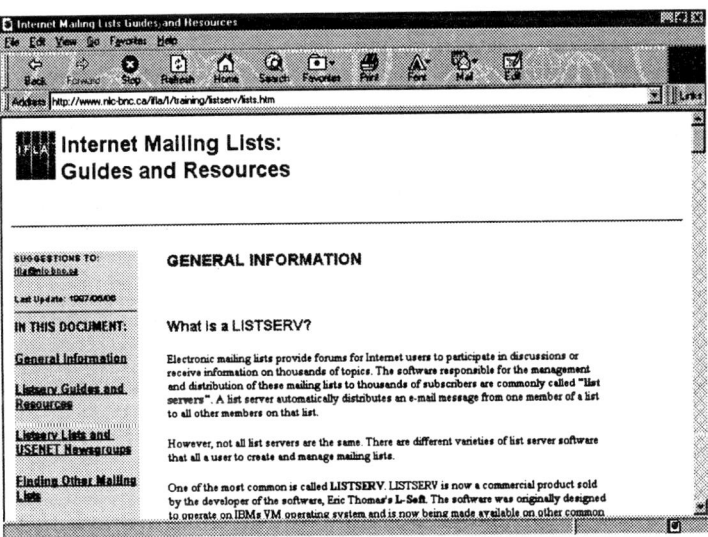

The FLA's Web site is an excellent information resource for those interested in email discussion groups

The sites below contain a searchable list of discussion groups, allowing you to look for email lists that cover your area of interest. These sites generally also provide instructions on how to join the discussion groups, or who to contact for more information.

Search the List-of-Lists:

http://catalog.com/vivian/interest-group-search.html

Liszt—The Mailing List Directory:
http://www.liszt.com/
List of Publicly Accessible Mailing Lists:
http://www.neosoft.com/internet/paml/index.html
Tile.Net Lists:
http://tile.net/lists/
L-Soft List Search:
http://www.lsoft.com/lists/list_q.html

Usenet

Usenet newsgroups are an excellent source of information - both in terms of FAQs and the willingness of Usenet participants to answer questions.

To participate in Usenet discussions, you generally need a newsreader program. If you use either Internet Explorer or Netscape Navigator as your Web browser, you have all that you need, as these both feature built-in newsreading capabilities. Check your manual or the program's online help for this information.

Failing this, you may need to download and install a special newsreader program.

There are a number available (usually free or shareware) for both Mac and IBM PCs. Alternatively, ask your Internet Service Provider or computer administrator to provide you with one.

Usenet newsgroups work in a similar manner to email discussion lists, with one vital exception.

TIP
You can also subscribe to mailing lists via a Web page, such as Mailing List Web Gateway (http://www.netspace.org/cgi-bin/lwgate). Simply search the list of available email discussion groups to find one of interest, then follow the onscreen prompts to subscribe.

When you create and post a message (known as an *article)* to a Usenet newsgroup, it is uploaded to a Usenet server.

Instead of being automatically distributed to everyone who reads that newsgroup, the article is stored online and can be downloaded by any participant. That is, each Usenet newsgroup acts like a noticeboard, and articles sent

Other Research Options

to newsgroups are displayed in a public forum which anyone with the appropriate newsreader software can read.

Given that Usenet newsgroups have a potential audience of millions, you can be confident that someone will help with your query, or at least point you in the right direction.

There are two ways in which another Internet user may respond to your question.

The participant can note your email address (which is usually automatically included in your article when you post it) and respond to you privately via email. Alternatively, s/he may compose an article in response, and post that to the newsgroup, so that both your question and the answer are available to other newsgroup participants.

To find out more about Usenet, visit these informative sites:

What is Usenet FAQ:

http://www.tezcat.com/~abbyfg/faq/what-is-usenet.html

The Newbies NetGuide:

http://www.newbies-netguide.com/usenet/intro.html

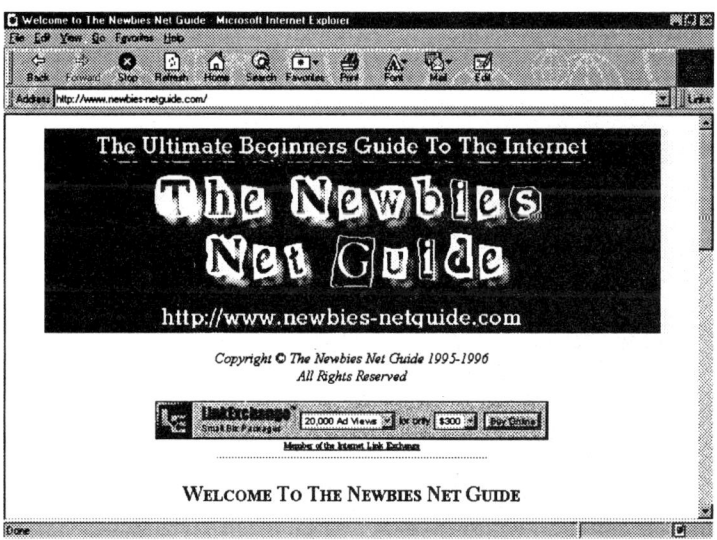

Zen & The Art of the Internet:

http://www.cs.indiana.edu/docproject/zen/zen-1.0_6.html

Déjà vu?

Not everyone is a dab hand at Usenet newsgroups. More importantly, not everyone has the time to follow one or more newsgroups in the hope of eventually finding the information they want. Often we need answers *now* - not tomorrow or next week.

There is an easier way to search Usenet newsgroups for articles of interest, and it is called Deja News.

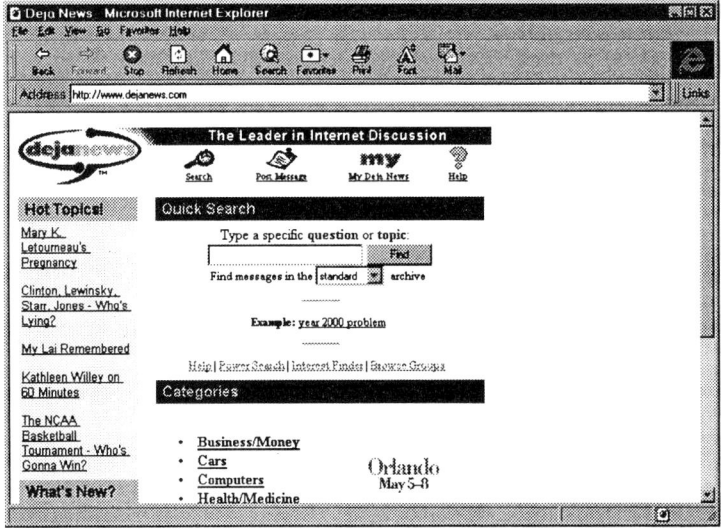

Deja News is a powerful search interface to Usenet newsgroup articles. It works in a similar manner to Search Engines, but instead of indexing Web sites, it indexes individual newsgroups and the articles posted to them.

TIP
Before you ask a question in either an email discussion group or a Usenet newsgroup, be sure to read any FAQs available in the forum. Most Internet users are happy to lend a hand, but it does rile people when they are faced with a user who has not made any attempt at researching the problem first.

Although most Search Engines allow you to search Usenet as well as the Web, none is custom designed to perform Usenet searches. This means that Deja News often has the advantage.

Deja News offers both a *Quick Search* and a *Power Search* interface.

With Quick Search, users type in their search terms (with or without operators) and click on the *Find* button.

Other Research Options 95

Deja News' Power Search interface (available via the Power Search icon in the navigation bar down the left side of the screen) gives users more control over the search process, including whether to perform AND or OR matching, whether to search through current or old news articles, and how matches and summaries should be displayed.

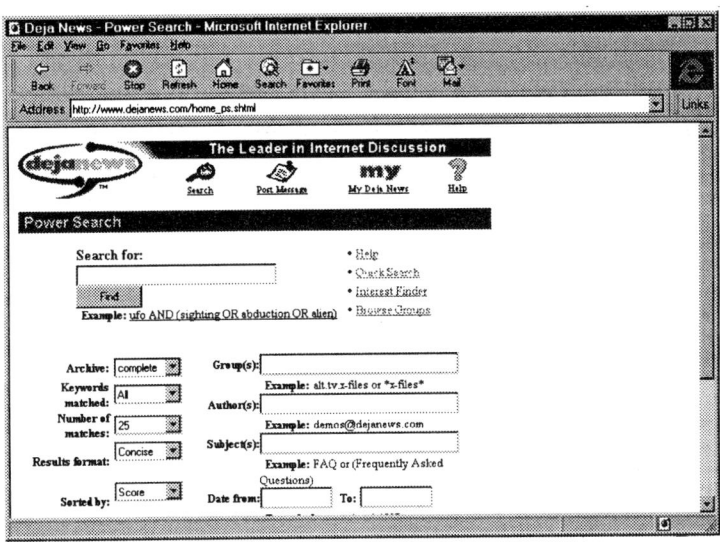

I performed a search using *cloning sheep* as my search terms. Admittedly, I was not entirely sure what Deja News would turn up.

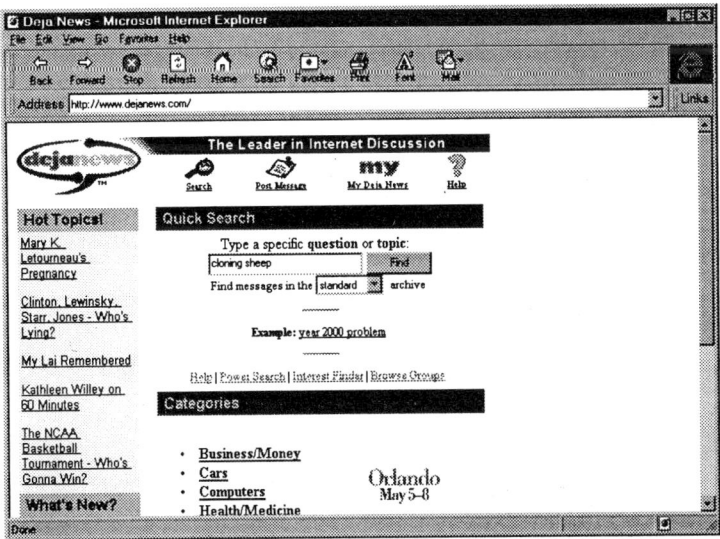

Deja News found 189 matches, in newsgroups ranging from *alt.religion.christ* (a religious discussion newsgroup) to *rec.humor* (a newsgroup for humour-related articles).

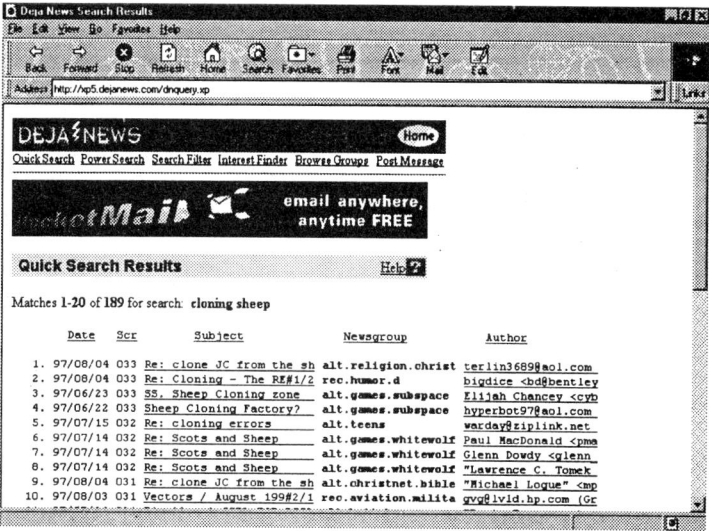

Deja News displays a list of matched articles, including details of when the article was posted, which newsgroup it was posted to, and who posted it.

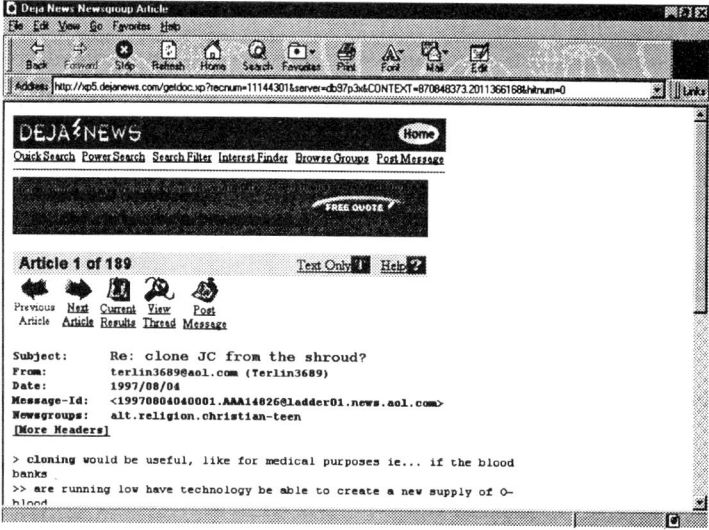

Once you have found a relevant article, Deja News lets you respond to the author or post your own message, just like a newsreader

Other Research Options

To read a particular article, simply click on the subject title. Deja News will display the full text of the article, and then give you the option of viewing any related newsgroup articles (via the *View Threads* icon) or posting your own response to the article you are reading (via the *Post Message* icon).

Deja News is a useful Usenet searching tool, allowing users to scan thousands of newsgroups for articles of interest to them - and all within seconds!

Virtual libraries

The resources discussed in this book are designed to make finding information on the Internet easy. But some people still may not find the information they want. This may be for a number of reasons - they might not be proficient at using search tools, they might not be couching their search queries in the right terms or, quite possibly, the information that they want might not be available online.

Whatever the reason, don't despair. You have one last port of call - a virtual library.

Virtual libraries, as their name suggests, are Web sites designed using the same principles as traditional libraries. As such, they tend to be carefully organised, extensively cross-referenced, and contain "hand-selected" materials which have been chosen on the basis of information quality.

There are a number of virtual libraries available online, but all tend to fit within one of two categories: general reference and specific reference libraries.

General reference libraries attempt to tie together the major resources available on the Internet, then categorise and catalogue them.

On the other hand, specific reference libraries seek to provide an exhaustive index of all online resources relating to a single, defined topic.

Which virtual library you use depends on what you are looking for, and how you prefer to search!

The Internet Public Library

The Internet Public Library is a true gem. The Web site might not be the most graphically oriented or intuitive site around, but it is expertly indexed into bite-size chunks.

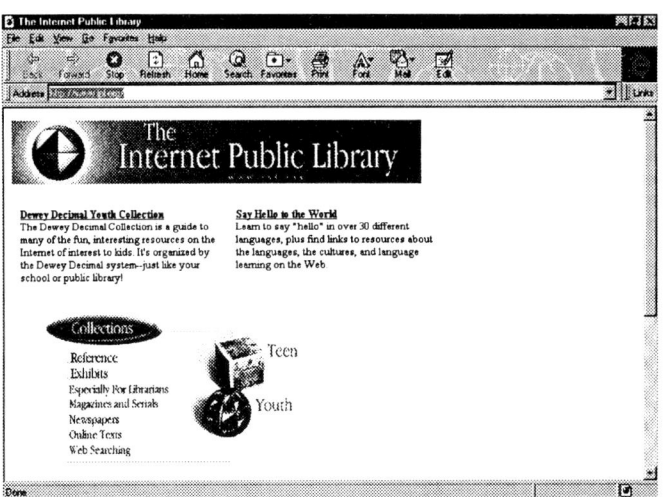

The Internet Public Library is about as good as it gets when it comes to organised information collections. See for yourself at http://www.ipl.org

All the categories available at the Internet Public Library site mimic a real library's layout. For instance, there is a reference section (with 2,093 items), a reading room (containing links to magazines and newspaper sites) and a text area (containing 5,820 items). There are also plenty of links to other electronic library sites and related resources.

The online text area warrants a special mention.

Not only can you browse by author, title or Dewey Subject Classification (as you would in a real library), but you can also search the text of the books using a simple search interface.

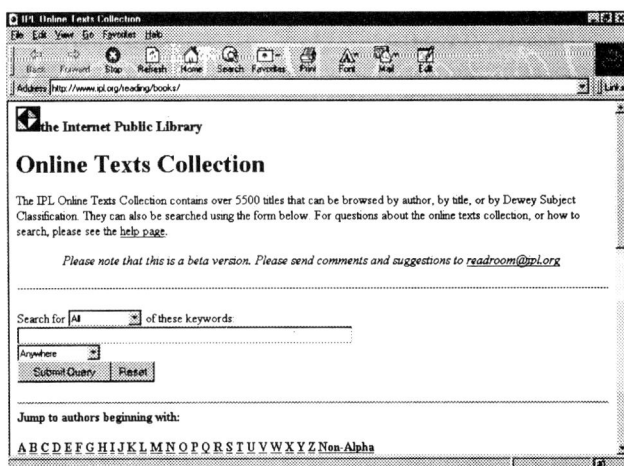

Berkley Digital Library

The Berkley Digital Library is designed to provide access to other online libraries and resources, as well as information and guidance for users who want to create an information resource themselves.

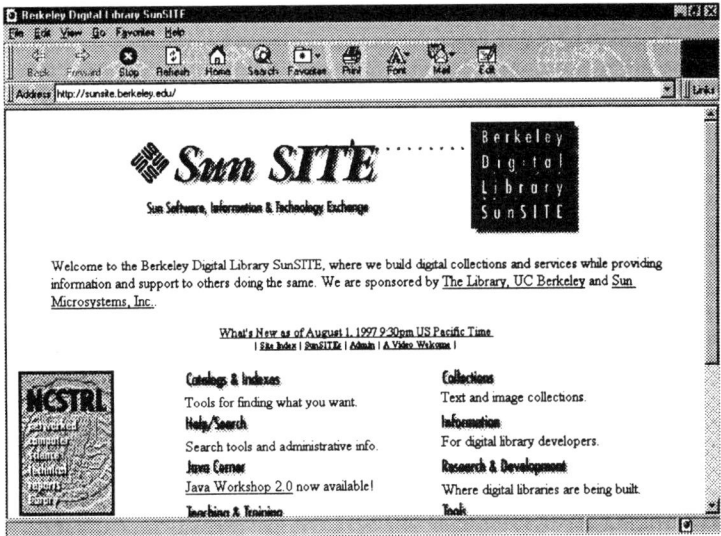

The Berkley Digital Library site (http://sunsite.berkeley.edu/) contains links to information about other online libraries and useful resources

It contains links to many other information repositories (including serials, papers and books), as well as guidance on how to use other search tools to find information online.

Librarians' Index to the Internet

The main page of the Librarians' Index to the Internet (shown on the following page) hosts links to areas such as *Law*, *Literature*, *Media* and *Geography*.

These main categories are divided into four or five sub-categories, all available on the main Web page, so that you can start searching in the right area straight away.

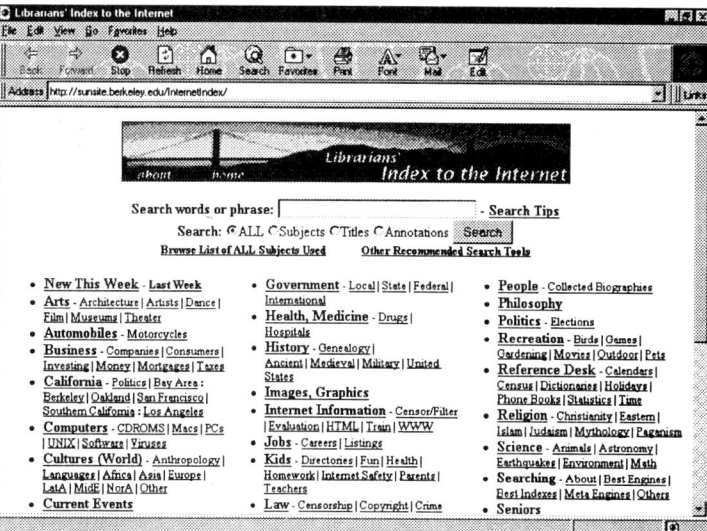

The Librarians' Index to the Internet—divided into many handy categories

When you select a subject area to view, a collection of sites will appear, each with a summary of its contents. Unlike Yahoo!, you won't find hundreds of sites in each category - but you can rest assured that the sites listed are well worth visiting.

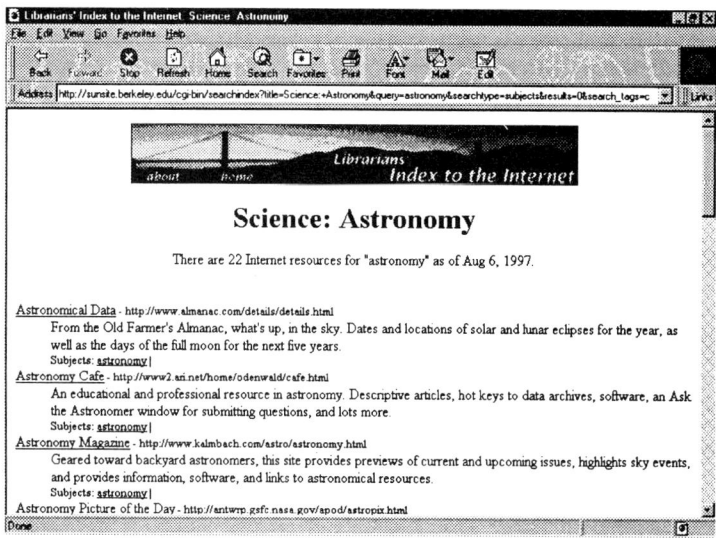

Each site within the Librarians' Index is chosen for its information value

Encarta Concise Encyclopaedia

Internet users can search the contents of Encarta online via the Encarta Concise Encyclopaedia Web site (shown on the following page).

Users type in a word or phrase, specify (optionally) a general area in which to search (such as *Religion, Life Sciences* or *History*) and choose whether matches should be restricted to articles, photographs or illustrations by toggling the appropriate boxes.

If you're just browsing, take a look at the Encarta online Schoolhouse. This page offers a selection of images, articles and interactivity to present and teach a topic (which changes at regular intervals). It is perhaps not so useful when you're searching for something specific - but fun all the same.

But perhaps the best feature of the Encarta Concise Encyclopaedia Web site is that all of its articles are cross-referenced via hyperlinks, making it easy to navigate related articles.

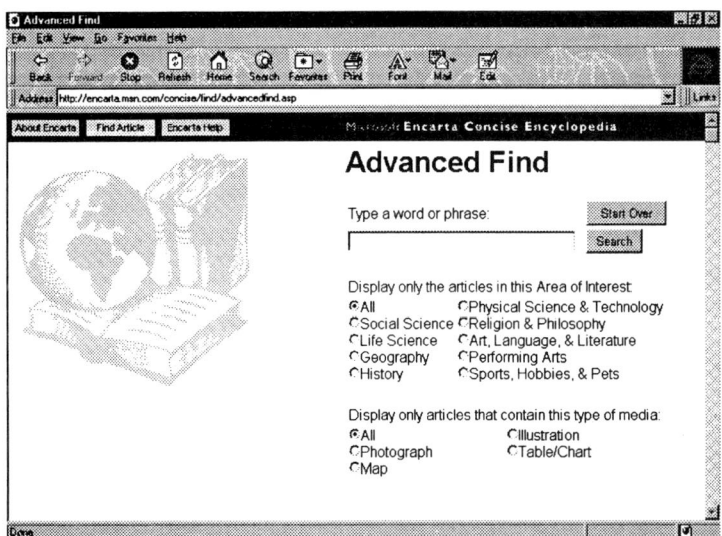

Search the Encarta Encyclopaedia online at http://encarta.msn.com/concise/find/advancedfind.asp

I performed a search for *Captain Cook*, and found several matches relating to his voyages throughout the Pacific Ocean, as shown on the next page.

102 Find What You Want on the Internet

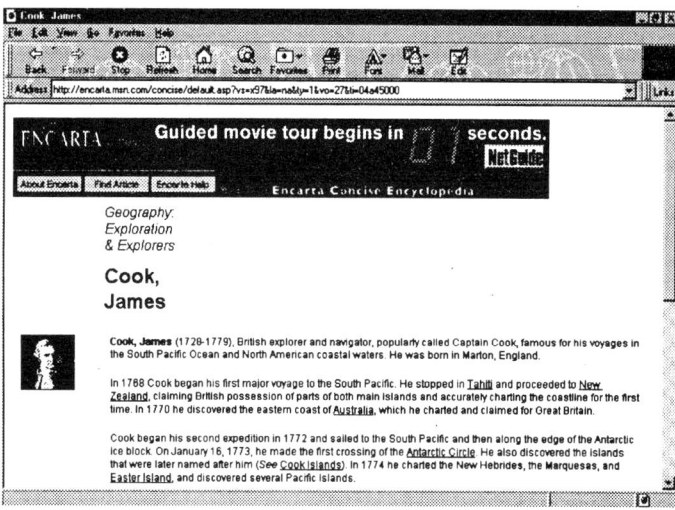

Finding information on Captain Cook is a breeze with the Encarta Web site

The WWW Virtual Library

Sometimes graphics and cute navigation features can hinder the search process. There is no risk of that at the WWW Virtual Library site, where graphics are kept to an absolute minimum.

The main Web page contains a lengthy list of subject areas.

Unfortunately, because minimal attention is paid to layout, you must scroll through several screens to read the entire list.

Alternatively, you can start with a (much shorter) Library of Congress catalogue of main subject headings (available via a hyperlink at the top of the main Web page).

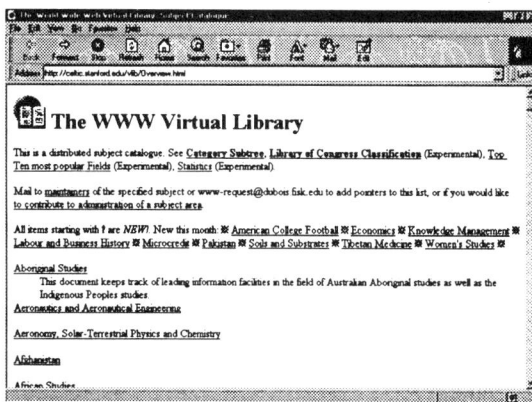

It might look ordinary, but the WWW Virtual Library packs a mean punch (http://celtic.stanford.edu/vlib/Overview.html)

Appendix

Search Engines and Software

There are hundreds of excellent Search Engines on the Internet. Unfortunately, this guide has only been able to canvass a handful. Below is a partial list of other Search Engines - some well known, others not - that you might like to explore for yourself:

Search Engines

Magellan:
http://www.mckinley.com/

OpenText:
http://index.opentext.net/

Polar Search:
http://www.polarsearch.com/english/index.html

Planet Search:
http://www.planetsearch.com/

What-U-Seek:
http://whatuseek.com/

I-Explorer:
http://www.i-explorer.com/

Galaxy:
http://www.einet.net/

Starting Point:
http://www.stpt.com/

Look Smart:
http://looksmart.com/

Matilda Search Engine:
http://www.aaa.com.au/

Nerd World:
http://www.nerdworld.com/

Web Wombat:
http://www.webwombat.com.au/

The Argus Clearinghouse:
http://www.clearinghouse.net/

Searches:
http://www.searches.com/

Other Meta-Search Search Engines

All-in-One:
http://www.albany.net/allinone/

C|Net Search:
http://www.search.com/

MotherLoad
http://www.cosmix.com/motherload/

SavvySearch
http://guaraldi.cs.colostate.edu:2000/

Starting Point Power Search:
http://www.stpt.com/pwrsrch/pwrsrch.html

Search Engine and Intelligent Agent software

Intelligent Agents

Below is a list of Intelligent Agents to download and play with:

Secret Agent:
http://www.ariel.co.uk/sagent

Web Retriever:
http://www.folio.com/retriever/

SmartSearch:
http://www.xilinx.com/

WebCompass:
http://www.quarterdeck.com/

Echo Search:
http://www.iconvex.com/

Net Attache:
http://www.tympani.com/

Search Engine companion programs

A number of Web Search Engines offer customised software which allows you to perform searches without running your Web browser. This can dramatically decrease search times, as you do not have to wait for images and so on to download. Below is a list of several such programs:

InfoSeek QuickSeek:

Works with both Internet Explorer and Netscape Navigator/Communicator, allowing you to search InfoSeek without first connecting to the site. Get your copy (PC or Mac) from:

http://guide.infoseek.com/iseek?pg=quickseek/Download.html

InfoSeek iSeek:

Search InfoSeek directly from your desktop, without a Web browser:

http://guide.infoseek.com/iseek?pg=iseek.html

HotBot's NewBot:

Works with Internet Explorer only, but currently supports Windows 95, Windows NT and Macintosh. Get your copy at:

http://www.newbot.com

Lycos Quicksearch:

Search Lycos from within your Web browser. Find details at:

http://www.lycos.com/software/software-search.html

Excite Direct:

Yet another Web browser add-on, which allows you to submit searches from within your favourite Web browser. To find out more visit:

http://www.excite.com/direct/

Desktop search software

There are a number of desktop search programs which will assist you in your searches for information online. Try these:

More Like This:

http://www.morelikethis.com/

WebSeeker:

http://www.ffg.com/seeker/

Internet FastFind:

http://www.symantec.com/trialware/index.html

Search Stream:

http://www.speed.inter.net/

WebFerret:

http://www.ferretsoft.com/

Glossary

Agent An Agent, also known as an Intelligent Agent, is a software program designed to search the Internet for information on behalf of a user. Agents search for information according to the requirements specified by its owner.

anonymous ftp The process of connecting to other computers on the Internet which allow public access (that is, which don't require you to have an account before you connect) in order to retrieve files stored on them. Connection is established using the ftp program, logging in with the username of *"anonymous"* and entering your email address as the password.

Archie A service available to all Internet users which is used to search for files or directories on other computers on the Internet which allow anonymous ftp logins. Once you locate the file, you can download it using your Web browser (see below) or an ftp program.

article The name used to refer to a message posted on the Usenet news system.

Boolean Boolean operators, AND, NOT and OR, are used to construct more accurate search queries, as these instruct Search Engines how they should treat or match search terms.

bps Bits per second. The speed by which modems are rated. This specifies the amount of data they can send and receive each second.

DNS Domain Name System. The system which regulates the naming of computers on the Net. The name and network address of every computer connected to the Internet is stored in a massive database which other computers access in order to translate computer names (such as domain.com.au) to numeric (IP) addresses (like 123.321.43.34).

domain name The official Internet name for a computer connected to the Internet. Your email address is comprised of your userid and the domain name of your ISP's computer, separated by the "@" symbol; ie. userid@domainname.

download The act of copying files from one computer (referred to as a "remote host") to your computer.

FAQ Frequently Asked Questions. A FAQ file is a compilation of questions and answers, designed to help newcomers to the Net. These can be found in Usenet newsgroups aimed at new users.

finger A program which allows you to determine if users are logged on, plus other useful information about them.

followup A reply to a Usenet posting which can be read by other Usenet readers. Newsreaders allow you to either reply directly to the author of a particular article (via email), or post your reply to the newsgroup for other subscribers to read.

ftp (1) The file transfer protocol: the standard which dictates the manner in which files are copied from computer to computer across the Internet; (2) The program used to copy files from one computer to another across the Internet.

Gopher A menu-driven interface used to find information on different computer systems. Usually accessed via telnet or a gopher client.

http hypertext transfer protocol. The protocol which regulates how information is transferred over the World Wide Web.

hypertext Documents that contain links to other documents. Hypertext forms the basis of the World Wide Web.

mailing list A list of email addresses of people who share a common interest. When you send an email message via a mailing list it is automatically copied and sent to every other person on that list.

moderator The person who scrutinises posts made to certain newsgroups, called moderated newsgroups, to ensure that they are accurate and on topic.

newsgroup The name given to each of the electronic notice or bulletin boards which comprise Usenet.

Query A query, commonly referred to as a search query, is one or more words submitted to a Search Engine or similar resource that define the information for which you are looking (the "search parameters").

Usenet The collection of thousands of electronic notice boards or discussion groups where information and ideas are exchanged on an endless array of topics.

upload The act of sending files or information from your computer to another computer, usually referred to as a remote host.

Web Robot A Web Robot, also known as a spider or crawler program, is a software program that explores and downloads the contents of individual Web pages in order to categorise and index them. Web robots are used by Search Engines to keep their databases up to date.

World Wide Web (WWW) A hypertext-based system linking information and files on different computers around the Internet. One of the most recent developments on the Internet, it allows users to browse information via an intuitive graphical user interface (GUI).

The Complete Beginner's Guide to Windows 95

This book isn't for the sort of people who get all frisky at the thought of a new operating system. They're already running Windows 95 and have been since day one. As the title suggests, it is for beginners:

❑ If you've just bought a new PC it will almost certainly be running Windows 95. You may need a helping hand to get started, and this book will serve as your introduction to Windows 95.
❑ If you've been using a PC with DOS or an earlier version of Windows and have decided to take the step up to Windows 95 this book will be a steadying hand to the new and to the different.
❑ If your office, school or college requires you to use a Windows 95 computer, this book will quickly show you the basics so you can get on with your work.
❑ Even if you're already using Windows 95 but simply want to do more with it, this book will teach you some neat tricks.

ISBN: 1-873668-28-7
Price: £4.95

About the Author
David Flynn is closely connected with Microsoft through his computer consultancy activities and is currently beta-testing early versions of the next Windows upgrade.

The Complete Beginner's Guide to Windows 95 is a low-cost, easy to understand guide, specially designed for everyone who hates wading through hundreds of pages of information to find a simple answer. **Order form on page 112**

Create Your Own Electronic Office

Home-based business... Cottage industry... Small Office/Home Office (SOHO)... whatever term you use, operating from home, means you escape the stresses, pressures and overheads of a busy town centre office. What-is-more, the time saved by not having to commute will allow you to work more efficiently and spend quality time enjoying yourself.

If this sounds like the kind of independence that you have dreamed of, then this book is for you. With its help, you will:

● Decide whether working from home is for you;
● Equip your office with the right technology to make it efficient from day one;
● Plan your new business and working environment

£5.95

Included are chapters on getting yourself motivated for working by yourself for yourself, how to maintain a healthy separation between your work and private life, and how to present yourself and your new business in a professional manner.

Complete Beginner's Guide to Word for Windows

Using Microsoft Word is a hit and miss process for a lot of people, and the end results are usually far from satisfying. What-is-more, many of the alternative books available are difficult to understand, and do not focus on the task of getting the job done, leaving you free to write creatively.

The Complete Beginner's Guide to Word for Windows is different. It has been designed and researched by the people who know best - the trainers who teach Word for a living. They understand both beginners and advanced students, and know how to meet their needs.

With clear, step-by-step instructions, and plenty of easy to understand examples, this book guides you to success the easy way. It leaves you free to concentrate on your document instead of getting the program to run properly! **£5.95**

Create Your Own Web Site

The World Wide Web is being transformed into an important business and communications tool. Millions of computer users around the globe now rely on the Web as a prime source of information and entertainment.

Once you begin to explore the wonders of the Internet, it isn't long before the first pangs of desire hit – you want your own Web site.

Whether it is to showcase your business and its products, or a compilation of information about your favourite hobby or sport, creating your own Web site is very exciting indeed. But unless you're familiar with graphics programs and HTML (the "native language" of the Web), as well as how to upload files to the Internet, creating your Web page can also be very frustrating!

£5.95

But it doesn't have to be that way. This book, written by an Internet consultant and graphics design specialist, will help demystify the process of creating and publishing a Web site. In it you will learn:

- What free tools are available that make producing your own Web site child's play (and where to find them);
- How to create your own dazzling graphics, using a variety of free computer graphics programs;
- Who to talk to when it comes to finding a home for your Web site (If you have an Internet account, you probably already have all that you need).

More Books from Net.Works

The Complete Beginner's Guide to The World Wide Web

Scott Western, an acknowledged, British, World Wide Web expert, leads you through every aspect of THE WEB highlighting interesting sites, and showing you the best ways to find and retrieve the information you want. Discover:

- ✔ How to minimise your time on-line, saving money for you or your company.
- ✔ Professional tricks for searching the Web
- ✔ How World Wide Web pages are designed and constructed
- ✔ All about domain names and getting your own web space

Price: £5.95

Tax Self Assessment Made Easy

Like it or not, the biggest change to the UK tax system has taken place. Self assessment is already in place for many taxpayers who may not even know it. Can it be ignored? No! New requirements for keeping records for example, or changes in the date for submitting tax returns will affect NINE MILLION people according to The Revenue. Penalties for not keeping records can be £3,000, whilst late tax returns can be charged at up to £60 per day.

Thankfully, Stefan Bernstein has distilled all the jargon down to a simple easy to follow guide **at a price the ordinary taxpayer can afford.** The book tells you what you have to do and when to do it, warning you of what happens if you don't.

ISBN: 1-873668-09-0   **Price:** £5.99

Making Money on The Internet

In 1996, businesses clocked up more than £350 million in sales over the Internet. Within one year that figure had risen to £500 million and was still growing almost exponentially!

These on-the-net businesses used the Internet to slash costs; decrease the cost of customer support; reduce purchasing costs; cut marketing expenses and to reach hitherto untapped markets. Their secrets are revealed in this book, so that you can make money on the Internet before your competitors beat you to it.

You'll find answers to the following questions:
- ● Is the Internet right for my business?
- ● How can I use the Internet to get and keep customers?
- ● Can I get started quickly and cheaply?
- ● What are the potential problems?   **Price:** Only £3.95

"highly recommend"
"An excellent publication."
Business Opportunity World

The Complete Beginner's Guide to The Internet

What exactly is The Internet? Where did it come from and where is it going? And, more importantly, how can everybody take their place in this new community?

The Complete Beginner's Guide to The Internet answers all of those questions and more. On top of being an indispensable guide to the basics of Cyberspace,

❑ It is the lowest priced introduction on the market by a long way at a surfer-friendly £4.95. Who wants to spend £30+ on an alternative to find out The Internet is not for them?

❑ It comes in an easy-to-read format. Alternatives, with their 300+ pages, are intimidating even to those who are familiar with The Net, let alone complete beginners!

Price: £4.95

The Complete Beginner's Guide to The Internet tells you:
- What types of resources are available for private, educational and business use,
- What software and hardware you need to access them,
- How to communicate with others, and
- The rules of the Superhighway, or 'netiquette'.

Book Order Form

Please complete the form USING BLOCK CAPITALS and return to
TTL, PO Box 200, Harrogate HG1 2YR or fax to **01423-526035**

❑ I enclose a cheque/postal order for £_____ made payable to '**TTL**'

Book	Qty	Price

❑ Please debit my Visa/Amex/Mastercard No:

Postage: Over £8 free, otherwise please add 50p per item within UK, £1.50 elsewhere **Total:**

Expiry date: ☐☐☐☐   Title: _____   Initials: _____

Signature: _____   Name: _____

Date: _____   Address: _____

Please allow 14-21 days delivery.

_____   Postcode: _____

We hope to make you further exciting offers in the future. If you do not wish to receive these, please write to us at the above address.

Daytime Telephone: _____

find